Contents

Preface to the third edition

For this edition I have rewritten the text extensively, as well as updating it. So many developments have overtaken its predecessor that radical reassessment and serious surgery were necessary.

As examiners point out, the emphasis in privatization questions in the 1990s is different from that of the 1980s. Now the emphasis is on:

- What has privatization achieved?
- Who have been the winners and losers?
- Does regulation of utilities work?
- Should natural monopoly networks have remained in the public sector?
- Can privatized markets be contestable?
- Is franchising as important as asset selling?

All these questions are addressed fully in the text. As always, constructive criticism – from teachers and taught – will be welcomed.

Bryan Hurl
Series Editor

the public sector

Third edition

Bryan Hurl
Head of Economics
at Harrow School

Series Editor
Bryan Hurl

Heinemann

For Geraldine, stern critic and mentor

Heinemann Educational Publishers
Halley Court, Jordan Hill, Oxford OX2 8EJ
a division of Reed Educational & Professional Publishing Ltd
MELBOURNE   AUCKLAND
FLORENCE   PRAGUE   MADRID   ATHENS
SINGAPORE   TOKYO   SAO PAULO
CHICAGO   PORTSMOUTH (NH)   MEXICO
IBADAN   GABORONE   JOHANNESBURG
KAMPALA   NAIROBI

First published 1988
Third edition 1995

98 97 96
10 9 8 7 6 5 4 3 2

British Library Cataloguing in Publication Data
A catalogue record for this book is available from the British Library

ISBN 0 435 33032 2

Typeset and illustrated by TechType, Abingdon, Oxon.
Printed and bound in Great Britain by Clays Ltd, St Ives plc

Acknowledgements

The publishers would like to thank the following for permission to reproduce copyright material:
Anforme Ltd for Figures 8 and 9 on p. 27; Associated Examining Board for the questions on pp. 23, 36–8, 49, 65, 85; Sir Gordon Borrie for the article on p. 68; British Telecom plc for the extracts from company reports on p. 66; Martin Cave for the extract on p. 81; © *Daily Mail*/Solo for the extract on p. 69; *Daily Telegraph* for the extracts on pp. 5, 6; © *The Economist* for the extracts and statistics on pp. 40, 64, 72; Eastern Electricity plc for the sales information on p. 89; *Financial Times* for the extracts on pp. 74–5, 86–7; Her Majesty's Stationery Office for the extracts from government expenditure plans pp. 37–8 and from Social Trends 21 on p. 50; Raymond Hoffenberg for the letter on p. 31; Nigel Lawson for the quotation on p. 25 and the extract from *The View from No. 11* on p. 88; Lloyd's Bank plc for the adapted extract from *Lloyd's Bank Review* on p. 10; Professor Sir Duncan Nichol for the letter on p. 31; Northern Examinations and Assessment Board for the questions on pp. 23, 36, 49–50, 65, 73, 86; *The Observer* for the extract on p. 88; Oxford and Cambridge Schools Examination Board for the questions on pp. 36, 65–6, 73; David Parker for the idea for Figure 14 on p. 54; Penguin Books Ltd for the extract from the *Penguin Dictionary of Economics* on p. 57; Graham Philpot for the cartoons on pp. 17, 48; Chris Riddell for the cartoons on pp. 67, 79, 85; David Simonds and *The Economist* for the cartoon on p. 26; David Smith for the extracts from *Studies in the UK Economy: UK Current Economic Policy* on pp. 30, 32, 53, 67; David E Smith for the cartoon on p. 71; *Sunday Express* for the extract on p. 88; Times Newspapers Ltd for the extracts from The Times on pp. 31, 88 and from the *Sunday Times* on p. 66; *Today* newspaper for the extract on p. 83; University of Cambridge Local Examinations Syndicate for the questions on pp. 9, 23, 36, 65, 73, 86; University of London Examinations and Assessment Council for the questions on pp. 9, 23–4, 36, 49, 65, 86; University of Oxford Delegacy of Local Examinations for the questions on pp. 9–10, 36, 49, 50–1; Welsh Joint Education Committee for the questions on pp. 74–5, 86–7; David Whynes for the extracts from *Studies in the UK Economy: Welfare State Economics* on pp. 28, 29; Richard Willson for the cartoons on pp. 39, 57.

The publishers have made every effort to contact the correct copyright holders. However, if any material has been incorrectly acknowledged, the publishers would be happy to make the necessary arrangements at the earliest opportunity.

Introduction

Textbooks of economics always offer a predictable contrast summary of the advantages and disadvantages of a free-market, *laissez faire*, economy versus a command, planned economy – before concluding, inevitably, that a mixed economy, one that attempts to combine the better features of both, is to be preferred. What tends to be omitted, however, is the observation that, in the UK's mixed economy, privatization is the policy which provides the battleground for the two political parties. As the *Economist* newspaper has observed:

'Traditionally, parties of Left and Right have fallen out over economics.'

This book shows why, how and with what result. Although the general public tends to think of privatization as synonymous with *denationalization*, were this to be true then the minting of new, linguistic currency and its widespread adoption in the 1980s could not have been justified.

Chapter 1 makes the case for the inclusion of deregulation and franchising, to cover the three aspects of this word. The prime minister and some journalists refer to franchising as 'semi-privatization'. Although not a headline grabber, as were the denationalizations of the 1980s, franchising is the privatization of the 1990s; a quiet revolution is taking place in the public sector. Meanwhile deregulation has created competition in the telecoms, gas and electricity industries formerly thought to be immune to such.

Chapter 2 considers the theoretical justification for a public sector based on market failure, specifically as a provider of positive externality goods and services whether public or merit, and as a redistributor of income. The economic reasons which were used to justify the nationalized industries are stated and their pricing problems, in theory, considered.

Chapter 3 makes a brief tour of public expenditure and revenue before introducing the peace dividend and the Welfare State reforms of rationing health care with internal markets. The Citizen's Charter and league tables feature. The performance and problems of the nationalized industries are examined.

Chapter 4 introduces the radical market reforms of the Tory governments, and the name Hayek. Efficiency, both productive and allocative, is defined and then – using Beesley and Littlechild's criteria – applied to the firms for privatization. Contestability and its relevance to natural monopoly utilities is looked at.

Chapter 5 is about regulation, and the regulators OFTEL, OFGAS, OFFER and OFWAT. Yardstick competition is defined. The price cap 'RPI minus x' is analysed and justified with regard to productive efficiency. The pricing problems facing the regulators are revealed – the peak load problem and price discrimination. Cherry-picking and regulatory capture are defined. The deregulation and structural reforms of the regulators to encourage competition are given due weight.

Chapter 6 is about privatization in the 1990s, defined as competitive franchising. Group 4's prison exploits are further publicized, along with market testing and the Next Steps programme. The contestable market for British Rail is unravelled, as are the 'dash for gas' and its relevance to the trade sale of British Coal.

Chapter 7 evaluates the micro and macro gains and losses of privatization and there is a summary Conclusion.

Chapter One
Privatization since 1980

'Selling off the family silver...' Lord Stockton

'Britain leads the world in privatization...'. My sceptical pupils react with surprise to this claim; they expect to hear *'used* to lead...'. But, if you turn to the lists of examples of UK privatization since 1980, on page 4 (Table 1), you will begin to understand why the Treasury claims that:

> *'In the UK the government's privatization programme has been one of the most radical economic changes since 1945.'*

Where we lead, others follow. Countries all around the world are actively pursuing privatization policies. The collapse of the **command economies** of eastern Europe and the former USSR means that these emerging democracies have to adopt privatization policies in order to establish some capitalism. An article in the *Economist* newspaper was pithy in its headline: 'EAST EUROPE FOR SALE'.

A new British export is expertise in the mechanics of privatization. The government, to encourage this, has established a 'know-how fund' for these countries, and City firms are marketing their skills in Poland, the Czech Republic, Slovakia and Hungary. From the political and economic chaos of the former USSR the emerging states are turning to privatization in the 1990s now that communism's command economy has collapsed.

The latest example of the export of Britain's expertise – consider its impact on the balance of payments – is *The Times'* headline on 20 September 1994:

> *Saudis seek help from Britain over privatization plans*

My pupils in the 1970s passed A level Economics ignorant of the word privatization. It was certainly not in their textbooks. Not until 1983 did the Penguin *Dictionary of Economics*, much used in schools, add to its third edition a definition along the following lines:

> **Privatization:** *The sale of government-owned equity in nationalized industries or other commercial enterprises, to private investors, with or without the loss of government control of the organizations.*

This would have been recognized by my pupils as a definition of **denationalization** whereby the government sold its **equity** – its notional shares as the owner of a public sector enterprise – so that shares could again be quoted, bought and sold on the stock market.

The *steel industry* was a shuttlecock that was used in the political knockabout game played between Labour and Conservative governments: it was nationalized, denationalized and renationalized. In 1988 the steel industry was denationalized. Or should we say it was privatized? What is the difference?

As privatization proceeds the legal experts who work for merchant banks, which the government uses to float the new issues of shares, invent new legal variations on the general theme. Cross Channel Hovercraft would slip through the net unless it is pointed out that the government gave it away....

The fifth edition of the Penguin *Dictionary of Economics* now has a subtle change to its privatization entry. The addition of one word to the original sentence tips the balance:

Principally *the sale of government-owned equity ... in these organizations. Other types of privatization may take the form of deregulation of a state-supported cartel or the subcontracting to the private sector of work previously carried out by state employees.*

Table 1 Examples of the 'sale of silver'*

Company	Date begun
British Aerospace	1981
Cable & Wireless	1981
Britoil	1982
Associated British Ports	1983
British Telecom	1984
Enterprise Oil	1984
British Gas	1986
British Airways	1987
Royal Ordnance	1987
Rolls Royce	1987
BAA	1987
British Steel	1988
Water (regional companies)`	1989
Electricity (regional companies)	1990
Electricity (generators)	1991

* The table is based on a narrow definition of privatization (i.e. asset sales of central government the proceeds of which were paid to HM Treasury after a public flotation). Refer to page 56 for examples of other types of sale, e.g. trade sale.

As the 1980s proceeded, the government denationalized an accelerating amount of 'silver'. So far it has raised £55 billion for the Exchequer. Table 1 is not an exhaustive list of all the sales; it is a summary of the major ones, some of which you should try to remember for examination purposes; for the latter the dates are not important, however. Another approach would be to summarize the transfers from state sector to private sector as steel, water, electricity, gas and telecommunications.

In the 1990s there is very little left in the privatization cupboard. At the time of writing, both coal and railways are being dealt with. This leaves Nuclear Electric and the Post Office, both of which are causing the government anguish because of perceived hostile public opinion. And yet notice the frequency of the topic in a representative broad-

Heseltine unveils Bill to sell off coal mines

MR HESELTINE, President of the Board of Trade, yesterday unveiled the Bill to privatize Britain's coal mines, saying they had become "an immense burden" on the public purse. Remaining pits will be offered for sale in five regional packages – Scotland, Wales, North East England and the central coalfields in two parts.

Some potential buyers had already expressed an interest, Mr Heseltine told a Westminster news conference. He stressed the need to open the industry to "market forces", but pledged that safety standards would remain "paramount" and miners' pensions protected.

Under the Bill, a coal authority will be established to issue licences to companies which win the bids, to give out information, and take control of responsibilities such as mining subsidence. Mr Heseltine said: "The coal industry has imposed an immense burden on public resources in recent years and it is essential that we should put it in a position where it can stand on its own as soon as possible."

He added: "Privatization represents the future for our coal-mining industry. It will free the industry from the restrictions of state control and give it an opportunity to compete effectively for its place in the energy market.

"Our aim is to achieve the largest economically viable coal-mining industry for the longer term while ensuring that the taxpayer gets value for money from the sale."

The Bill comes in the wake of the Government's controversial pit closure programme, which has made thousands of miners redundant.

Mr Heseltine has insisted that the closures were inevitable because the market for coal is shrinking, and he said yesterday he could not predict the state of the market in three or five or 10 years' time.

The Health and Safety Executive and HM Mines Inspectorate would retain responsibility for mines safety regulation and inspection.

Pensions and concessionary fuel entitlements of British Coal employees, both past and present, would be safeguarded.

Daily Telegraph, 3 December 1993

Rail sell-off could add to road chaos

Road traffic into London and other major cities could rise by a quarter as a result of rail privatization, according to a study by University College, London, *writes Charles Clover, Environment Editor.*

The Survey is based on an assumption by the consultants, Coopers & Lybrand, that Network SouthEast will have to raise rail fares by 65 per cent – in the "worst case" – as a result of expected shortfall in public funding.

The estimate of 28 per cent traffic growth is the extreme example but it does show that *any* shortfall in funding for rail or decline in service is likely to mean more people driving into major cities, with attendant environmental problems.

The study by Mr Martin Mogridge of UCL is based on reduced public spending on railways, from £1.5 billion a year to £740 million by 1997, announced in the Budget. According to consultants' estimates, privatization will mean £500 million added to the cost of running the network.

Ms Lynn Sloman of the environmental group Transport 2000, which commissioned the research, said "These are worst-case figures and very preliminary but they are also very worrying."

Daily Telegraph, 13 December 1993

sheet, the *Daily Telegraph*; two articles within ten days.

As the cupboard emptied, so the government's economic advisers widened the net of privatization – which is why the dictionary, quoted above, widened its definition. As believers in the superiority of the market mechanism and its virtuous 'invisible hand', they argued for **deregulation,** the removal of statutory barriers to market entry, and for **franchising.** This is where the public sector continues to *provide* because it finances the services, but *production* shifts to the private sector. Figure 1 summarizes this three-point definition of privatization.

So the classic quotation, as the heading to the chapter, from Lord Stockton, begins to look less than accurate: it is hardly appropriate for deregulation or franchising. But it became a cliché of the critics of Margaret Thatcher's privatizing governments of the 1980s. They accused her of *selling the family silver to subsidize a riotous living,* claiming that, rather than raise taxes or cut public expenditure, her governments sought to gain revenue for tax cuts from what the Left called *the privatization swag.*

What is the economic truth of this supposed irresponsible prodigality? A full answer will have to wait until Chapter 7, but it is worth complimenting the phrase in the quotation as a piece of political rhetoric. Selling the silver is a headline grabber, or in TV terms, a 'sound bite' – but as economics the phrase is less than satisfactory.

If you sell off your family silver to spend on an irresponsible spree

Denationalization: the sale of public sector assets

As well as nationalized industries this also includes companies and local authority council houses. Table 1 summarizes the major sales so far by the UK Treasury. It omits the proceeds from council house sales which go directly to the councils concerned.

Deregulation (a synonym is *liberalization*): the removal of legal barriers to entry to a previously protected market to allow private enterprise to compete

Public sector provision (financing) and public sector production are replaced by private provision and private production. Examples are bus services, telecoms, gas and electricity production.

Franchising: the public sector continues financial provision but for private sector production

Competitive tenders are requested for a contract to be awarded for a stated time period. Examples are contracts for NHS hospital meals and laundry, local authority refuse collection, and supervision of prisons.

Figure 1 A three-point definition of privatization

you very obviously lose the silver. If, however, the state sells off 'our' silver we do not lose it – it stays in the family because we are all part of the same family. If you used nationalized gas and telephones before privatization then you now use them still – from British Gas plc and British Telecom plc. Neither the gas nor the telephone system have disappeared.

It would be much more appropriate to discuss the merits or otherwise of redistributing the family silver amidst a greater number of the family, since this has produced economic changes of great importance. The proceeds of privatization have benefited particular groups and there may be conflicts of interest. The merchant banks employed by the government to float and underwrite the issues have made huge profits along with the related institutions that worked on these over-publicized flotations. These institutions have been very happy to take their part of the 'swag'. Selling deliberately under-priced shares has created a new breed of stock market gambler and source of capital gain income. Shares over-subscribed ten times sounds more like the Roaring Twenties and the world of Scott Fitzgerald. **Equity** is a vital concept in economic theory: there will be more to say on this subject in the next chapter. It should not be confused with *share equity* but understood to involve *fairness*.

Confused ignorance

Two of the earliest definitions you were taught in economics are supposed to help you distinguish between **positive** economics, the facts, and
normative economics, people's opinions. Would that this were so easy;
the subject of privatization is a minefield of claim and counter-claim.

If your teachers do succeed in persuading you to read about contemporary economic events – both because they are intrinsically interesting, and, if your self-interest has to be appealed to, because the exam
boards now expect, in the new syllabuses, a mix of theory and applied,
contemporary knowledge – you will quickly fall victim to pressure
groups unless you are on your guard.

A **pressure group** is a body which wants to influence government or
some authority which has the power to introduce change favourable to
it. In economics you should already be aware of:

- the **CBI** (Confederation of British Industry) whose Director General
  and other spokespersons feature in the media to put forward the
  views of business people
- the **TUC** (Trades Union Congress) whose General Secretary propa-
  gates in the media the views of the trades union movement.

In general the CBI will look more favourably on a Conservative government and the TUC more favourably on a Labour one. And there, in a
nutshell, is a perfect example of a normative divide, since political
divides tend to be based on economics. Beware the all-too-predictable
TV 'debate' featuring politicians. Instead of a reasoned consensus in
many areas you get a Punch & Judy show of 'bash the opposition'.
Good TV? The programme schedulers think so. Good economics?
Sadly, confused ignorance is the outcome. Note especially the letters on
page 31; are the 'facts' genuine?

Current privatization issues which are generating more heat than
light are:

- Should British Gas be broken up as recommended by the
  Monopolies amd Mergers Commission?
- Should the Post Office be privatized?
- For the privatization of British Rail the government is trying to
  make the passenger services contestable through franchising. Critics
  say the method will hit the buffers.

Who is right? At A and AS level your answers score higher marks if you
can identify these divides and itemize the arguments for and the arguments against. Positive economics is the order of the day. Now read on to
see whether this book is an unbiased presentation of positive economics.

```
                          KEY WORDS

    Command economies          Positive
    Denationalization          Normative
    Equity                     Pressure groups
    Deregulation               CBI
    Franchising                TUC
```

Reading list

Beherell, A., 'Privatization – success or failure?', *Economics Today*, Anforme, Sept. 1994.

Smith, D., Chapter 9 in *UK Current Economic Policy*, Heinemann Educational, 1994.

The Treasury, *Privatization*, Economic Briefing no. 1, 1990.

Essay topics

1. (a) To what extent is the distinction between free market and centrally planned economic systems still relevant in the real world? [40 marks]

   (b) What economic role now exists for government? [60 marks] (University of London Examinations and Assessment Council 1993)

2. (a) Explain what privatization is.

   (b) Do you support the trend towards privatization found in many economies? (University of Cambridge Local Examinations Syndicate 1994)

Data Response Question 1

Energy strategy

This task is based on a question set by the University of Oxford Delegacy of Local Examinations in 1994. Read the passages below and then, using the material of the passage and your knowledge of economics, answer the questions which follow.

Extract 1

Before privatization the electricity companies were the captive customers of British Coal. In 1975 three-quarters of Britain's electricity was produced from coal, now that is due to fall back to less than a third.

The opening up of the energy market to the cold winds of competition and private sector forces means that the electricity generators are free to choose other sources like gas, oil and cheap imported coal. Faced by such a dramatic fall in demand, British Coal has had no alternative but to close down its more uneconomic pits (*coal mines*), with the loss of 30,000 jobs. The knock-on effects could swell the total to 100,000.

Source: adapted from 'Did the pits have to shut?', Tom McGhie and Nick Fletcher, *Sunday Express,* 15 October 1992

Extract 2
A common characteristic of the privatization schemes for industries which, for many years have been managed by state corporations, is that uneconomic activities are brought out into the open. In the case of coal, 'uneconomic' pits would become a major issue following a programme of privatization.

'Uneconomic' pits would not necessarily be closed; the decision would depend on the estimated costs and benefits to society of keeping them open. Some people have gone so far as to claim that practically all pits should be kept open until physical exhaustion, on the grounds that, in times of high unemployment, the 'shadow' wages of miners is close to zero. Thus pits should not be classified as 'uneconomic' on the basis of British Coal's costs as such pits would appear to be 'economic' on this social accounting basis.

Source: adapted from 'A liberalized coal market', Colin Robinson, *Lloyd's Bank Review,* April 1987

1. (a) What do you understand by the term 'privatization'? [2 marks]
   (b) Outline *two* arguments in favour of privatization. [4 marks]
2. Using economic theory, carefully explain the reasoning behind the following quotations:
   (a) British Coal has had no alternative but to close down its more uneconomic pits' [4 marks]
   (b) '…with the loss of 30,000 jobs. The knock-on effects could swell the total to 100,000'. [4 marks]
3. Contrast the term 'uneconomic' in the second paragraph of Extract 2 with its use in Extract 1. [8 marks]
4. Briefly comment on *three* economic factors, not discussed in the passage, you would consider in deciding whether to keep open loss-making pits. [3 marks]

Chapter Two
The public sector in theory

*'... the common ownership of the means of production, distribution
and exchange ...'*
Clause 4 of the constitution of the Labour party, 1918–95

The economics of the mixed economy

In Britain's **mixed economy** some goods are provided by private capitalism in markets with a price mechanism and some are provided by central and local government in the non-market sector. The **nationalized industries** operated in the market sector but their assets were publicly owned; they merit a separate section shortly. We shall first examine four economic arguments for the mixed economy.

● First, without government intervention there will be *market failure*, where public and merit goods will be under-provided. When the 'right' bundle of these is provided then *social benefits* are gained by society in general, as well as by the individual consumer. These are **externalities**: public sector sewerage schemes remove epidemics, contagious diseases are reduced, the black death becomes of historical, rather than topical interest. A state-educated workforce is more productive than an illiterate one.

● Secondly, economics texts make much of the virtues of the price mechanism, as we shall see shortly, in evaluating privatization. But a defect is that **desired demand** is of no economic consequence in a market; only **effective demand**, backed up by purchasing power, qualifies. Adam Smith's oft-quoted 'invisible hand' does not acknowledge the price mechanism's inability to record compassion: it can produce mink coats for the rich but not children's shoes for paupers. **Income redistribution**, which Robin Hood practised illegaily and modern governments legally, is a mark of a caring society – we have now returned, as promised in Chapter 1, to the concept of *equity*.

Unequal factor endowments produce, inevitably, unequal incomes and wealth in a capitalist society; were this society *laissez faire* – non-interventionist in the sense that government withdraws from the provision of merit goods, transfer payments and subsidies – then the distribution of income could well become $L_1L_2L_3L_4$ on the **Lorenz curve** (see Figure 2). This curve shows the relationship between the cumulative

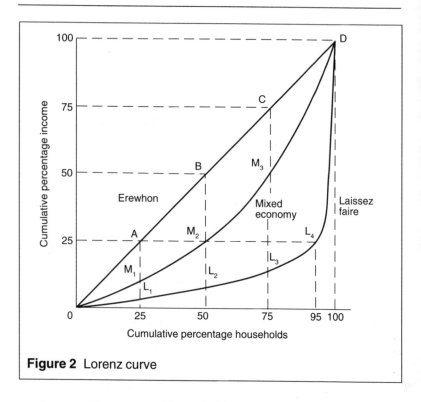

Figure 2 Lorenz curve

percentage of incomes and households such that, in a perfectly egalitarian society, 25 per cent of households at A would have 25 per cent of incomes; and at B, 50 per cent of them would have 50 per cent of incomes. We shall call this Erewhon, an anagram of Nowhere. A *laissez faire* society would have gross disparities, as at L_4 where the top 5 per cent are very rich with 75 per cent of income because 95 per cent of households only have 25 per cent.

A mixed economy with a prominent public sector shifts the curve to M_1, M_2 and M_3, using income taxes, wealth taxes, transfer payments and subsidies. Public sector goods and services provide part of a household's **standard of living**. Household X with two children at a state school, one of whom needs frequent NHS medical attention, has a higher **social wage**, income in kind, than household Y, a healthy bachelor schoolmaster with the same net money income. X consumes education and health; Y, who is fit and active, neither.

Privatization can change the distribution of incomes if firms prosper after their asset sales, and the distribution of wealth if those who buy the privatized shares find that their value rises. For buyers of privatization shares 'silver' turns to gold.

The largest saleable assets were the nationalized industries because they operated in markets with prices whereas public and merit goods are deliberately not priced to the final consumer.

Public goods

A **public good** is a good or service that is impossible to price to an individual consumer. If it is to be provided for some it has to be provided for all. As it is impossible to prevent anybody from consuming it, free riders could consume without paying, so capitalism is reluctant to supply it – it is *non-excludable* from the point of view of the seller. Public goods prevent a market system from generating an optimum allocation of resources.

A public good is an externality. The benefit people get depends not only on how much they have but also on how much other people have. Yet two individuals need not place the same value on marginal amounts because their marginal utilities differ. Public goods confer positive, benefiting externalities. The marginal cost for supply to an additional consumer is zero.

Public 'bads' confer negative externalities, which include polluted air, crime and poverty. A government, through legislation, can create a clean air zone and so change a public bad into a public good. Public expenditure on a judiciary and the police force reduces crime.

Additionally, a public good is *non-rival*. When household A consumes it this does not stop household B consuming it, simultaneously. On the other hand the word processor that is printing this sentence was purchased in a market, at a price; it is a normal good which is both *excludable* and *rival*. It was provided by a firm which aimed to make a profit, to one buyer whose consumption of it prevented others buying it.

A favourite example of a public good is lighthouses. Textbooks state that you could not build a lighthouse near dangerous rocks and charge passing mariners for the service you offer them. How would you prevent 'free riders', consumers unwilling to pay, because payment is so easily avoidable? As early as 1974 Ronald Coase dismissed this textbook cliché. Evidently 'light dues' were collected from ships at ports; lighthouses were built, operated, financed and owned by private enterprise.

So we try again: a colleague of mine is an energetic member of the CND movement and on occasions we have had spirited disagreements. Defence is one of the rare examples of a pure public good, and the nuclear deterrent – which I wanted until the collapse of communism and he did not – is only available collectively. My colleague cannot opt out as an individual; collectively we have it or collectively we do not. Those who regard such as a disbenefit are 'reluctant riders'. Now I have become a reluctant rider since communism's collapse.

It is rare to find a pure public good. Because of congestion both roads and police can be partly rivalrous in consumption. Most examples are impure public goods: they have a private goods element. *It is not part of the definition of a public good that it be publicly provided.* While it is impossible to use a market system for most roads it is more than feasible to privatize the Severn Bridge and the Dartford Tunnel because they *are* excludable – the continental members of the EU are great believers in motorway tolls. Drivers could be charged for using the M25.

The BBC and the independent television companies provide non-excludable broadcasting. The BBC is in the public sector, funded by a licence fee due from all set owners. Commercial sponsors provide ITV, so a public good is in the private sector. It would be possible to privatize the BBC. Furthermore, with the deregulation of broadcasting since 1992, cable television further muddies the economists' classifications: cable TV is metered to the individual user so this form of broadcasting is a private good that is excludable.

Merit goods

Merit goods are goods which some people think others should consume more of. They are rival goods, and they are excludable. However, they confer both direct private benefits as well as external collective benefits.

A market for them could exist; private enterprise could offer them at a price, but insufficient would be consumed according to some social judgement. The **Welfare State** provides NHS prescriptions at a nominal market price and schools and hospitals at no market price. A cherished belief of social reformers is that households would underprovide for themselves, in a market. For the low-paid, paying monthly health insurance premiums could be prohibitive.

Note the direct conflict with the economist's assumption that households are rational utility-maximizers, the arbiters of their own consumption. Laws against the consumption of **demerit goods**, e.g. heroin and glue sniffing, call this into question. Compulsory seat-belt wearing saves lives. The state becomes paternalistic – it takes on the role of father-figure to decide for you, it becomes the Universal Provider State, it provides security, i.e. sick pay, unemployment benefit, pensions, health care, housing and education. Unfortunately this means that the state becomes a near monopoly provider of these services, because there is limited competition from private hospitals and fee-paying independent schools. 94 per cent of children consume state education for which there is no market charge.

If your parents had to pay for you to attend school, would they buy the best at a price or go for a cheaper one so that a better car and frequent continental holidays could also be consumed by your household? Incidentally the gain you are deriving from being educated includes making you a better citizen, so do you agree that education can be classified also as an externality?

● A third justification for government intervention is an extension of the externality argument already used, fashionably called 'green' taxes. Governments have realized that they can present these as 'useful' taxes, their aim being to correct the specific market failure of overproduction of a good or service which exacts a cost on the environment. Susan Grant discusses green taxes in her companion volume in this series, *Fiscal Policy*.

● Finally, as Adam Smith observed more than 200 years ago:

> '*People of the same trade seldom meet together, even for merriment and diversion, but the conversation ends in a conspiracy against the public, or in some contrivance to raise prices.*'

Two hundred years later nothing has changed except that firms have become more sophisticated in their 'anti-competitive practices'. This is the official phrase from current **competition policy** legislation, along with concern for 'the public interest', and is a further function of government. It legislates and produces bodies to protect consumer interests, such as the **Director General of Fair Trading** and the **Monopolies and Mergers Commission**. Both of these will feature later because of the contribution they can make to the public interest where privatization has produced the potential for consumer exploitation. The regulators who have been established to supervise the privatized utilities can call in the MMC, when in dispute, to act as referee. See especially Chapters 5 and 6.

The socialist view of nationalized industries

These are public sector enterprises that produce and sell goods in the market economy. They arise from the ideology of socialist governments. The epigraph at the start of this chapter is a classic quotation from the Labour party's membership card. In full Clause 4 reads:

> '*To secure for the workers by hand or brain the full fruits of their industry and the most equitable distribution thereof that may be possible upon the basis of the common ownership of the means of production, distribution*

and exchange and the best obtainable system of popular administration and control of each industry or service.'

As is common in texts of this nature I acknowledge its normative standpoint and therefore endeavour to concentrate on less controversial positive economics. In passing, however, note again the reference to *equity* – '...the most equitable distribution...'. Philpot's cartoon reproduced here features the famous loaves and fishes economic problem and seems to sum up perfectly the left-wing view. Incidentally, what are the factory chimneys doing in the cartoon?

The major NIs of the post-war period were nationalized by the Labour governments of 1945 to 1951. Their ideology is above; their economic arguments were as follows.

Economic arguments for nationalized industries

• Externalities

These can confer positive social benefits, but they can also impose negative **social costs**. A market price evaluates only the private cost to the producer and the excludable, rivalrous private benefit to the purchaser. Its production may, however, be imposing unrecorded social costs on non-consumers.

'Acid-rain' – the fallout from emissions of sulphur dioxide from power station chimneys – pollutes the atmosphere, is carried by the prevailing winds and falls on the European continent, visibly affecting buildings and the northern coniferous forests. A nationalized electricity industry could be instructed by the government to install costly filtration equipment to improve the standard of living of our EU partners. Loss-making rural bus services are kept in existence on government orders. British Rail has loss-making lines which it keeps open because they confer social benefits.

If loss-making is institutionalized then deficit financing requires Exchequer grants to cover the shortfall. When a firm is forced to calculate external costs as well as internal, it *'internalizes'* the externality and charges a higher price for its product.

• Redistribution of income

This is administratively easy if the **public utilities** – gas, water, electricity, telephone – are nationalized. These essential, basic, household needs can be priced below cost to reduce the cost of living.

Internalizing externalities is also a way of redistributing income, but this could be regressive: note the policy conflict between this argument and the preceding one on negative externalities.

Is profit next to ungodliness?

● Natural monopolies

Natural monopolies are created in a market where only one supplier is the inevitable outcome. Duplicate pipelines beneath roads for household gas supply would be economically wasteful. The **public utilities** are natural monopolies: that have **economies of scale**, falling average and marginal costs, with greater capital input and product output. Consumers benefit if prices are correspondingly lower.

In Figure 3 the market is supplied, initially, by many firms and their aggregate market supply curve is S_c. This competition produces price P_c where supply and demand are equal at C. If, after mergers and takeovers, a natural monopolist emerges, capable of achieving economies of scale, then the new marginal cost curve (MC_m) produces, even with profit maximization, at W, where $MC_m = MR$, a higher quantity Q_m and a lower price P_m. These are the gains for the consumer from a monopoly.

The gains from economies of scale from **network** or **common carrier** natural monopolists who own gas and electricity grids and telephone lines can be compromised by the opportunity for monopoly profit and the powerful barrier to entry to potential rival firms wanting to use the network and offer lower prices. The incumbent monopolist can use vertical integration and predatory pricing as 'anti-competitive practices'. Anxiety over this behaviour possibility was an economic reason for nationalization. Privatization in the late 1980s sparked much opposition and forced the government to address this problem with

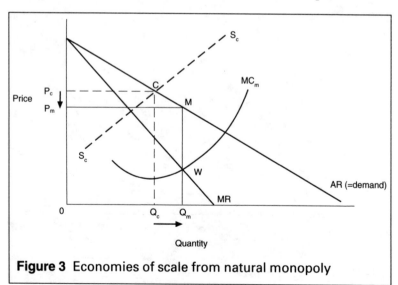

Figure 3 Economies of scale from natural monopoly

safeguards for the public interest, with the establishment of regulatory bodies to police these industries.

● Profit maximization

A profit-maximizing, private sector, natural monopolist would redistribute income from consumers to shareholders because it would choose a higher price, if in an unregulated, *laissez-faire* business environment.

It would choose an output where the marginal cost equals the marginal revenue, at point W in Figure 4. The shaded rectangle P_wRFT shows the profit. Note the downward-sloping curves which indicate economies of scale: to reduce the AC the MC must be below it. As there is a sole supplier, the AR curve for the monopolist is society's market demand curve; it is, therefore, downward-sloping. With output Q_w and with MC equal to MR, then the appropriate price is horizontally from R on the demand curve. The AC is cut at point F, so the total cost OTFQ$_w$ is less than revenue.

A nationalized natural monopolist could be instructed to give the monopoly profit to the Exchequer for the betterment of its public sector shareholders – society in general. But is output Q_w optimizing society's resources, and is price P_w the 'right' price?

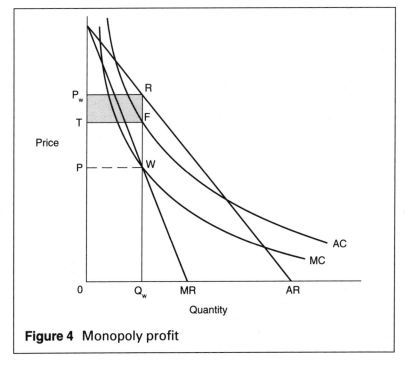

Figure 4 Monopoly profit

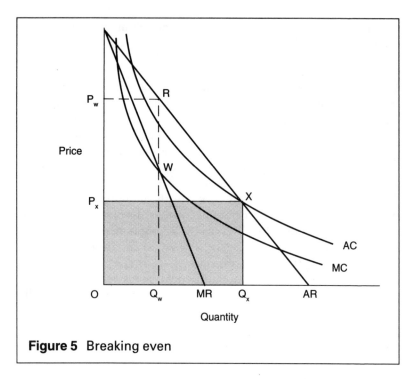

Figure 5 Breaking even

● Breaking even

Alternatively the NI could be instructed by the government to 'break even' (i.e. to cover costs but not make any excess, monopoly, profit). In Figure 5 demand is no longer at R, on the demand curve, but expands to X because of the lower price P_x. X marks the break-even point where revenue, OP_x times OQ_x, equals costs, OQ_x times XQ_x. Consumers get a greater output, Q_wQ_x extra, at the lower price, P_wP_x smaller.

However, factor markets will need to supply extra resource inputs for this, for which there will be an **opportunity cost** – the output foregone from the next best alternative use. What is the 'best' use from the economist's standpoint of economic efficiency?

● Price equal to marginal cost

A third possibility is to set P equal to MC at Y, in Figure 6, conforming to a cherished ideal of economic theory. Let us see why.

If the demand curve is a true reflection of society's evaluation of a good – subject to warnings of inequitable income distribution and the market's rigid need for effective, not desired, demand – then the price is equal to the marginal utility (MU) of the last unit consumed. Prices

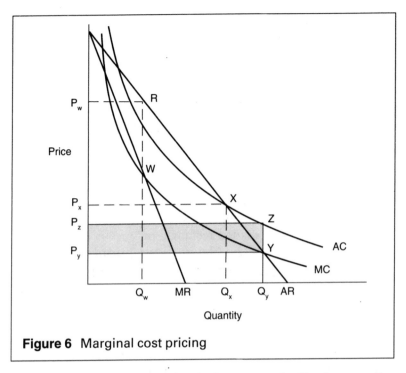

Figure 6 Marginal cost pricing

are not on a sliding scale to reflect higher marginal utility for preceding quantities: consumers gain a **consumer surplus** on these.

   If the marginal cost curve is a true reflection of society's evaluation of the resource opportunity cost of supply – subject to warnings of distorted evaluation if social costs and benefits are omitted – then the price, *if it is equal to MC*, shows that

$$P = MU = MC.$$

Adam Smith's virtuous 'invisible hand' price mechanism produces a balanced equation of demand equals supply. Hence

$$MU = MC$$

for the last unit demanded and for the last unit supplied.

   Moreover, the opportunity cost may be important because society wants an **optimal output** of competing goods and services, requiring scarce factors of production as inputs. Then, in a two-product world (a and b), where

$$\frac{P_a}{P_b} = \frac{MU_a}{MU_b} = \frac{MC_a}{MC_b},$$

an optimal balance exists. To transfer resources from a to b, or from b to a, sub-optimizes society's benefits from its factors or production.

Conclusions

What does all this imply for the public sector?

- There are no market prices for public goods nor for most public sector merit goods. We wonder what is the optimal quantity to supply, the right input of scarce factors of production to use.
- For nationalized industries, it is clear that the monopoly profit with price OP_w in Figure 4 gives a price greater than MC by the magnitude PP_w. The optimization rule is not achieved.
- When P = MC at Y in Figure 6, optimization is achieved, but the falling AC curve of economies of scale leads straight into a very nasty problem. The shaded rectangle of surplus cost is above market revenue OP_yYQ_y. Marginal-cost pricing causes large deficits. *It provides loss-making nationalized industries.*

The theory has thrown up some tricky problems for the mixed economy and for economists. We want an efficient and equitable allocation and distribution of resources. Do we use markets or government? The post-war consensus held government to be superior for certain goods, these being public goods, merit goods and natural monopolies. However, the same problems still arise: how can we know what consumers want; how can we produce without inefficiency; what is an efficient quantity? The 'common ownership of the means of production' can create a lot of problems.

KEY WORDS

Mixed economy	Competition policy
Nationalized industries	Director General of Fair Trading
Externalities	Monopolies and Mergers Commission
Desired demand	Social costs
Effective demand	Public utilities
Lorenz curve	Natural monopolies
Standard of living	Economies of scale
Social wage	Network
Public good	Common carrier
Merit goods	Opportunity cost
Welfare State	Consumer surplus
Demerit goods	Optimal output

Reading list

Burningham, D., and Davies, J., Chapter 2 in *Green Economics,* Heinemann Educational, 1995.

Grant, S., Chapter 2 in *Fiscal Policy*, Heinemann Educational, 1994.

Whynes, D., Chapters 1 and 2 in *Welfare State Economics*, Heinemann Educational, 1992.

Wilkinson, M., Chapters 2 and 6 in *Equity and Efficiency*, Heinemann Educational, 1992.

Essay topics

1. What economic reasons are there for state ownership of a particular industry? Given that an industry is in state ownership, what pricing policy should it be made to adopt? (University of Cambridge Local Examinations Syndicate 1990)

2. (a) Explain with the aid of examples the main characteristics of (i) public goods and (ii) merit goods. [5,5 marks]
   (b) To what extent is it desirable that the government should provide (i) public goods and (ii) merit goods? [6,9 marks] (Associated Examining Board 1994)

3. (a) 'A public sector provides public goods'. Is this a sufficiently accurate definition of a public sector? [12 marks]
   (b) Consider whether the public sector should be more concerned with macroeconomic policy or microeconomic policy. [13 marks] (University of Cambridge Local Examinations Syndicate 1993)

4. Explain what is meant by the term 'natural monopolies'. To what extent does the extension of privatization to cover some of the 'natural monopolies' in the UK constitute a problem for consumers and government? (Northern Examinations and Assessment Board 1994, AS level)

5. (a) Explain what is meant by an externality. [30 marks]
   (b) Examine the impact of introducing any two of the following: (i) pollution taxes, (ii) legal minimum controls on pollution emissions, (iii) tradeable pollution licence permits. [70 marks] (University of London Examinations and Assessment Council 1994)

Data Response Question 2

Pricing problems in a nationalized industry

This task is based on a question set by the University of London School Examinations Board in 1989. The firm represented in the diagram is nationalized and follows a marginal cost pricing policy.

1. With specific reference to the diagram, comment on the relationship between price elasticity of demand and marginal revenue.
2. What price would a nationalized industry charge and what output would it produce if pursuing a marginal cost pricing policy?
3. State the change in price that would occur if the firm were to adopt an average-cost pricing policy.
4. (a) What is meant by 'consumer surplus'?
   (b) Assume (i) the firm is now privatized and, instead of following a policy of marginal cost pricing, it follows a policy of profit maximization; and (ii) cost conditions are unchanged and the firm charges the same price to all consumers. What is the change in consumer surplus?
5. Subsequently, if this firm were to pursue a policy of price discrimination, explain with the aid of a diagram how profits could be increased.
6. Examine the circumstances in which a nationalized firm following a marginal cost pricing policy would incur a loss. Use a diagram to illustrate your answer.

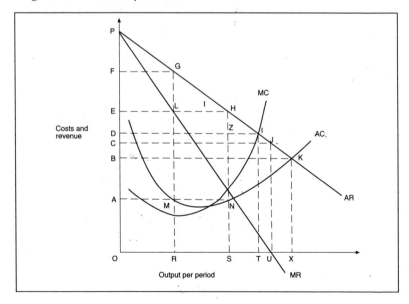

Chapter Three

The public sector in practice

'There is no utilitarian calculus that permits the numerical comparison of the benefits of, say, an extra military aircraft as against a new hospital. In the end there has to be a political decision.'
Nigel Lawson, when Chancellor of the Exchequer

Preliminaries

Since the establishment of the Welfare State and the majority of the nationalized industries in the immediate post-war period, economic problems have changed and so have attitudes. After offering so many false cures, our economic policy-makers have now turned their attention to a critical evaluation of the public sector.

A basic economic problem for them is that, if the public sector grows bigger as a proportion of the GDP, then private sector consumption, investment and exports are correspondingly lower unless economic growth is sufficiently large to allow the private sector to increase *absolutely* while this *relative* shift takes place.

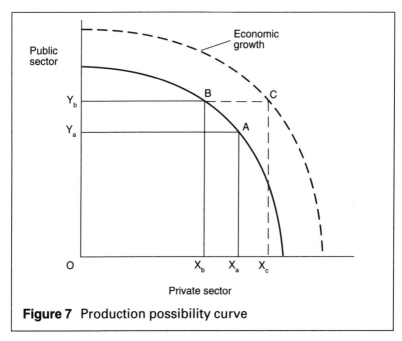

Figure 7 Production possibility curve

Figure 7 is a schematic **production possibility curve** at full employment output showing the trade-off between the shares of output for the public versus the private sectors: in media language, shares of the *national cake*. If the proportion of the GDP for the public sector rises, then the shift from A to B reduces the private sector by $X_a - X_b$. Correspondingly the public sector share rises by $Y_a - Y_b$ as resources are shifted into it.

If economic growth is positive then it *is* possible to have the national cake and eat it – in the sense that a shift from A to C gives more public sector output as well as extra $(X_a - X_c)$ private sector output. There is no trade-off, no direct opportunity cost, in the sense that one must fall to allow the other to rise.

The peace dividend

Finding itself increasingly under financial pressure in the 1990s as the public sector borrowing requirement spiralled out of control, the government started to seek a return from the **peace dividend**. With the ending of the Cold War and removal of the military threat from the former Communist bloc, the UK government can now reduce spending on military goods to switch to other public sector needs.

David Simonds's cartoon shows an axe being taken to military spending. The government, ever mindful of pressure groups and public opinion, especially when redundancies are inevitable, has chosen more deco-

rous language with its White Paper **Options for Change**. Actually the Old Testament foresaw the opportunity cost aspect of Options for Change 2000 years ago; Micah 5 reads:

> '*...and they shall beat their swords into ploughshares and their spears into pruning hooks; nation shall not lift up sword against nation, neither shall they learn war anymore; but they shall sit every man under his vine and under his fig tree.*'

Nigel Lawson's assertion at the start of this chapter is usually true; however, in this case the peace dividend could provide a '*utilitarian calculus*' which *replaces* military aircraft with hospitals.

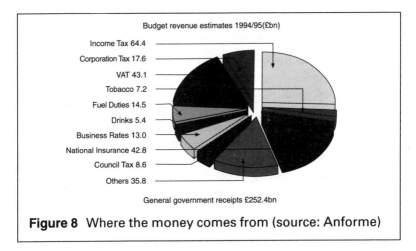

Figure 8 Where the money comes from (source: Anforme)

Public revenue and expenditure

The chief sources of revenue are:

- income tax
- VAT
- National Insurance contributions.

Even so, despite the projected receipt of £252 billion for 1994/95 (see Figure 8), pressure on public spending mounts. The big spenders are (see Figure 9):

- social security   - education
- health   - defence.

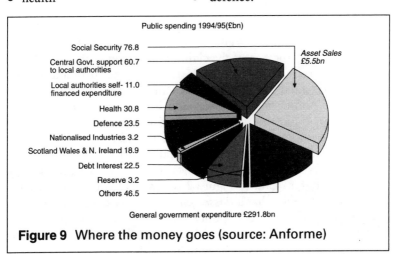

Figure 9 Where the money goes (source: Anforme)

THE WELFARE STATE

Economists use the term 'welfare state' to refer to those social welfare services in the economy which are organized and provided by the government. In the UK, the four principal types of welfare service are:

- cash benefits concerned with the relief of poverty, arising from, for example, unemployment, sickness or old age – these benefits are generally referred to as 'social security';
- public sector primary, secondary and higher education;
- health care provided by the National Health Service (NHS), and related personal social services, such as residential care of the elderly and social work;
- public sector housing, and cash benefits to assist indviduals with housing costs.

Source: Whynes, D., *Welfare State Economics*

With further tax rises politically unpopular, and the peace dividend unable to deliver sufficient revenue every year, the government has been forced to two other courses:

- selling assets (the 'family silver') to the public
- reforming the Welfare State and other parts of the public sector to increase efficiency and rein back the inexorable growth of public sector expenditure.

The importance of the Welfare State in the modern UK economy can be gauged by the size of the claim it makes on both government and national resources. In 1994/95 the social security and health budgets represented over 50 per cent of all direct central government expenditure. Adding education accounts for 22 per cent of GDP.

At this stage you should look back to the previous chapter and make some economic classifications. Health and education are *merit* goods. Defence is a *public* good. Social security is the functional name for *transfer payments*. The government robs rich Peter to pay poor Paula. Refer again to Figure 2 on page 12, the Lorenz curve, and remind yourself what a *laissez faire* economy does *not* do for its sick, unemployed, retired or poor. They are expected to turn to the markets and take out insurance policies, or otherwise they hope for charity.

SIR WILLIAM THE GIANT-KILLER

The Welfare State came into being as the result of the ideas and efforts of a great many people. However, if any one person can be identified as the principal architect of the Welfare State in Britain then it is surely Sir William Beveridge (1874–1964). Beveridge was Director of the London School of Economics between 1919 and 1937, and then Master of University College, Oxford. He became a government advisor during the Second World War and, briefly, a member of parliament, before accepting a peerage and Liberal leadership in the House of Lords. To a greater or lesser extent, he made a contribution to every area of social policy which was implemented in the 1940s and 1950s.

Beveridge described the necessary road to social reconstruction after 1945 as an attack on five giants, whose names were 'Want, Disease, Ignorance, Squalor and Idleness'.

- The attack on ignorance was to be led by the 1944 Education Act, of which Beveridge was co-sponsor.
- Disease was to be defeated by the creation of the National Health Service.
- Idleness was to be overcome by the government's 1944 White Paper commitment to maintain 'a high and stable level of employment' by means of Keynesian economic management techniques.
- Squalor was to be addressed by the support of incomes, by housing development and by environmental planning.
- Beveridge's most sustained personal efforts were directed towards the attack on want, in the form of his book *Social Insurance and Allied Services*, published in 1942. Known to this day simply as the **Beveridge Report**, it laid the foundations of the modern system of unemployment and sickness insurance, known in the 1990s as social security.

Source: Whynes, D., *Welfare State Economics*

The 'giant killer'

As the box above shows, Want was one of the five giants that the architect of the Welfare State, Sir William Beveridge, wanted to slay with social security income transfers. Ignorance can be slain by the merit good, free state education; Disease by the NHS; and Squalor by provision of subsidized council housing.

Since 1950, social security spending has risen sevenfold, *in real terms*; since 1980 growth has averaged 3 per cent a year *excluding the payment of unemployment benefit* for the millions of unemployed. As David Smith wrote in *UK Current Economic Policy*:

> *'The delivery of the services that comprise the welfare state has been widely perceived to be of poor quality, bureaucratic in nature and failing to meet the needs of customers.'*

Figure 10 shows how welfare spending, as a percentage of GDP, is rising inexorably, especially on social security and health.

Rationing health care

Ask a member of the Christian church to price a life and the reaction is likely to be one of hostility towards the insensitive economist seeking a 'utilitarian calculus'. To a Christian, 'everyone's life is priceless in the eyes of God'. Unfortunately, economists have to ask such uncomfortable questions because to say that rationing does not exist is to deny reality. Many doctors, bound by their Hippocratic oath, denounce rationing as immoral. The Bishop of Birmingham has attacked the current NHS reforms, which we are about to study, as

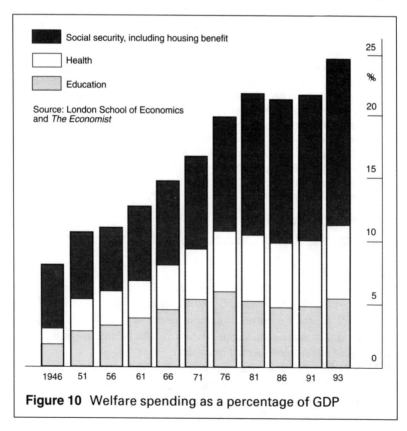

Figure 10 Welfare spending as a percentage of GDP

'un-Christian'. The following information may help to put the problem in perspective.

Rationing health care is an economic fact of life. If provision is free at point of consumption the predictable outcome is that demand will exceed supply. In all OECD countries health care provision is under increasing resource pressure because of:

- ageing populations – life expectancy has risen
- rising costs of health technology
- rising expectations from the consumer, e.g. for organ transplants.

Yet the public suffers 'confused ignorance' from media sensationalism – see page 8. The need for greater general awareness of the choices required is highlighted by the following letters to *The Times*.

From Professor Sir Duncan Nichol and others

Sir, We write to announce the formation and plans of Healthcare 2000. Whilst debate continues over the Government's NHS reforms, and whether they are working to the benefit of patients, we feel there is a need for a longer-term perspective.

We are concerned that the pace of medical and technological advance, together with rising consumer expectations, will create an increasing mismatch between demand for better healthcare and the resources available. The challenge of balancing resources and demand will be the same, regardless of which government is in power.

What is needed is an open debate about fundamental issues such as the quality and method of delivering services, the rationing of those services, consumer choice and how services should best be funded to secure optimum healthcare at a cost that the public are willing and able to afford.

We intend to examine the many contributions to the health debate thus far and invite all participants in the process – consumers, professionals, managers, staff, economists and politicians – to contribute their experience and views to a debate about the long-term issues in health and healthcare.

DUNCAN NICHOL
(Professor of Health Services Management, University of Manchester)

From Sir Raymond Hoffenberg

Sir, I welcome the initiative of Sir Duncan Nichol's group. However, it should be recalled that the main reason for the "mismatch between demand for better healthcare and the resources available" is the parsimony of spending on the NHS over the past ten or fifteen years.

What was once widely regarded as a superb health system was systematically eroded by underfunding that has put our spending very close to the bottom of the OECD league. If we were to spend simply at the average OECD level, we could defer the need for serious rationing for a very long time indeed.

I am dismayed to read that the group feels an open debate is needed *now* about such fundamental issues as the delivery of services anbd how best they should be funded. Why didn't this take place five years ago before Mrs Thatcher so precipitately introduced her drastic and damaging so-called "reforms"?

Instead of "get ready, take aim, fire" the Government chose "get ready, fire, take aim". How sad it is that, five years down the road, Sir Duncan's group still doesn't know whether the changes "are working to the benefit of patients". Exactly who has benefited from the experiment?

R. HOFFENBERG
(President, Royal College of Physicians, 1983–89), 2 Mulberry Court, Field House Drive, Oxford.

Critics of the NHS reforms have dubbed them as reckless marketization. They are certainly *not* privatization. A market price for health and education is feasible but would be electoral suicide for the government involved.

Internal markets in the Welfare State

An academic revolution in economic theory has been put into practice by successive Conservative governments since 1979. The public sector has been privatized where possible. The Next Steps initiative, called 'semi-privatization' by the media because it involves compulsory, competitive franchising for public provision but private production,

---

INTERNAL MARKETS

Perhaps the most far-reaching change of all in the Welfare State has been the move to introduce internal markets. In the NHS, general practitioners have been encouraged to become 'GP fundholders', with the size of their budget depending on the number of patients registering with them. The GP's role has changed. If he or she has a patient requiring hospital treatment, the choice will be between competing hospitals (with an increasing number of these operating as NHS Hospital Trusts), on the basis of price, quality and the length of time the patient will have to wait for treatment. The market not only directs patients towards the best and most competitive GPs and hospitals but it also constrains spending in two important ways. GPs, knowing that the profit of their practice depends on it, have an incentive to prescribe the cheapest available (usually generic) drugs. Hospitals need to hold down their prices to survive.

The state education system has also developed an internal market. Under the Local Management in Schools (LMS) initiative, schools have been encouraged to opt-out of local education authority control. The success of opted-out schools depends on their ability to attract pupils. To provide users of state education with the means of choosing between competing schools, testing has been introduced. Thus, pupils will be directed to schools offering the best quality, as defined by test results and other measures. As in any other market, those that do not offer a good service will go out of existence.

Source: Smith, D., *UK Current Economic Policy*

---

pushes further the revolution. Finally, 'almost privatization', the introduction of internal markets replaces state monopoly providers with competitive, state ones. Sometimes called a 'quasi-market', an internal market differs from a conventional one because:

- there is no profit maximization on the supply side – what should state-funded schools and hospitals maximize?
- on the demand side there is no price, so how can consumer sovereignty arise?

In both health and education the direct consumer needs an agent as purchaser – your parents for your choice of education, and a doctor or medical expert because you are not informed enough to know what is wrong with you. The final customer is not involved directly as a purchaser, in either case.

The basis of the reforms is a purchaser/provider split. The former is the demand side; the latter, the supply side. Your budget-holding GP has to shop around: he or she will evaluate NHS Trust hospitals which have taken over their own financial affairs. The money is still provided annually by the state. The doctor has new information, or **performance indicators:**

- death rates for hospital patients
- waiting lists
- hospital star ratings based on (i) casualty patients assessed within five minutes of arrival, as a percentage, (ii) outpatients seen within 30 minutes of appointment, (iii) percentage of operations not requiring overnight stay.

This is all clearly derived from the concept of the **Citizen's Charter,** into which prime minister John Major invested a lot of his political capital. Every household received a copy. It reads:

> 'The Citizen's Charter is about giving more power to the citizen. I want the Charter to be one of the central themes of public life in the 1990s'.

The Charter has four aims:

- work for better quality in every public service
- give people more choice
- make sure everyone is told what kind of service to expect
- make sure people know what to do if something goes wrong.

There is a danger that administrative costs may offset efficiency gains. Although still in its infancy, the GP fundholders and competitive schools look encouraging. There is anxiety over the equity aspect of hospitals.

The nationalized industries

These are public sector enterprises that produce and sell goods in the market economy. The NIs had a central role in the economy before privatization. In 1979 they produced more than 9 per cent of the GDP, nearly 12 per cent of capital investment and employed 8 per cent of the labour force.

Privatization aimed to transfer one million jobs to the private sector and reduce the state industry GDP contribution by half. In 1979 they dominated the energy, communications, steel and transport sectors. To a Labour politician they represent '*the commanding heights of the economy*', which the Left would wish to retain in the public sector.

Table 2 itemizes the nationalized industries and public sector firms in rank order of turnover, inherited by the privatizing Conservative administration of 1979. There are additions at the end: the Bank of

Table 2 The nationalized industries and public sector firms in 1979; all subsequently privatized except for *

Nationalized industries by rank order of turnover
    Electricity
    British Telecom
    British Gas
    National Coal Board (since renamed British Coal)
    British Steel
    British Aerospace
    British Rail
* Post Office
    British Airways
    British Shipbuilders
    National Bus Company
    National Freight Corporation
    British Airports Authority

Renamed corporations
    Britoil (formerly BNOC)
    Enterprise Oil (formerly owned by British Gas)

Miscellaneous firms
* Bank of England
    Rover Group (British Leyland): a quoted company but traded with
       government subsidies
    Rolls Royce
    Ferranti
    Cable & Wireless
    Amersham International
    Johnson Matthey Bank (added 1984)

England which was nationalized in 1946, but is not regarded as an NI; and a clutch of firms, most of which were nationalized by accident rather than by design after they went bankrupt in the market, but were taken over as public assets to keep them trading. Rolls Royce was a celebrated example, and the Rover Group continued to trade with the help of large government subsidies.

Purists would argue, rightly, that the list has been doctored for ease of assimilation. British Telecom and the Post Office were combined in a single corporation until 1980. Britoil and Enterprise Oil did not exist as separate legal entities in 1979; they were renamed for flotation as privatized corporations.

Tarnished silver?

Much criticism had built up by 1979 from economists dissatisfied by the performance of the nationalized industries.

- In theory governments were supposed to adopt an 'arm's length' approach, leaving the managers to get on with day-to-day entrepreneurial decisions. In practice, governments meddled and public interest was sacrificed to the government's self-interest.
- The Treasury struggled to assert commercial aims for the NIs, and White Papers in 1961, 1967 and 1978 outlined financial and commercial guidelines but these always came second-best to the government's needs.
- Such interference, and the lower salaries for the top managers compared with private sector employment, meant that the top-calibre entrepreneurs shunned the NIs.
- Richard Pryke made comparative studies of services where they were provided by both public and private sectors. He found public services inefficient:

   'What public ownership does is to eliminate the threat of takeover and, ultimately, of bankruptcy and the need to raise money in the market. … Public ownership provides a comfortable life and destroys the commercial ethic.'

Evidently the 'family silver' sold off in the 1980s (Table 2) was very tarnished.

KEY WORDS	
Production possibility curve	Beveridge Report
Peace dividend	Performance indicators
Options for Change	Citizen's Charter

Reading list

Anderton, A., Unit 6 in *The Student's Economy in Focus*, Causeway Press, annually.

National Institute of Economic and Social Research, Chapter 3 in *The UK Economy*, 3rd edn, Heinemann Educational, 1995.

Propper, C., 'Incentives in the new health care market', *Economic Review*, Feb. 1993.

Smith, D., Chapter 3 in *UK Current Economic Policy*, Heinemann Educational, 1994.

Whynes, D., *Welfare State Economics*, Heinemann Educational, 1992.

Essay topics

1. What economic reasons are there for state ownership of a particular industry? Given that an industry is in state ownership, what pricing policy should it be made to adopt? (University of Cambridge Local Examinations Syndicate 1990)

2. (a) Explain how the price mechanism assists in the allocation of resources. [12 marks]
   (b) Discuss the case for and against doctors (GPs) charging patients for their services. [13 marks] (Associated Examining Board 1993)

3. (a) With reference to public expenditure, distinguish between current expenditure, capital expenditure and transfer expenditure. [30 marks]
   (b) What factors may explain changes in (i) the total level, and (ii) the composition, of public expenditure over time? [40 marks]
   (c) Examine the problems involved in attempting to control public expenditure. [30 marks] (University of London Examinations and Assessment Council 1993)

4. 'The National Health Service has effectively been privatized'. Discuss (Oxford & Cambridge Schools Examination Board 1994)

5. What impact has the introduction of competition and the operation of market forces had on the National Health Service in the UK? To what extent is it possible to measure the efficiency of a hospital? (Northern Examinations and Assessment Board 1994, AS level)

6. (a) What are the conditions necessary for the efficient functioning of a market economy? [8 marks]
   (b) Why, in the cases of (i) environmental protection and (ii) street lighting is provision not left to the free market? [6,6 marks] (University of Oxford Delegacy of Local Examinations 1994)

Data Response Question 3

The nationalized industries

This task is based on a question set by the Associated Examining Board in 1990. Study the tables and analysis and answer the questions at the end.

In 1979, the nationalized industries accounted for about 9 per cent of GDP and 11.5 per cent of investment. They employed over 1.7 million people. Since then, the privatization programme has substantially reduced the state-owned sector of industry. Nonetheless, those industries still in public ownership remain a major presence in the economy, accounting for 5 per cent of GDP and 6 per cent of investment, and employing just over 750 000 people. The industries' performance is thus of considerable importance for the country as a whole.

The accompanying tables show the changes in productivity (output per person employed) and the operating profits of those industries which were in the public sector at 31 March 1989.

The financial controls on the nationalized industries have been built on the arrangements which were set out in the 1978 White Paper *The Nationalized Industries*. The control framework operated at a number of levels:

- *Strategic objectives* are agreed with each individual industry.
- *Financial targets and performance aims.* Financial targets, usually set for three year periods, are the primary control on the industries.
- *External financing limits* (EFLs) were introduced in 1976 as a short-term control on the amount of finance, whether grant or borrowing, which an industry may raise during the financial year to supplement the income from its trading activities.
- *Investment appraisal and pricing principles.* Most nationalized industries are required to aim at a rate of return on their new investment programmes of 5% in real terms. This is intended to ensure a proper return on investment in the industries and, at the same time, that the industries do not divert resources away from areas where they could be used more effectively. It is set taking into account the pre-tax rates of return achieved by private companies.
- *Monitoring* plays an important part in stimulating and controlling the industries' performance in the interests of the taxpayer and consumer.

Source: *The Government's Expenditure Plans,* 1989/90 to 1991/92

Table A Nationalized industries' productivity

	Annual percentage changes		
	Nationalized industries	All manufacturing industries	Whole economy
1978–79	3.5	1.8	1.8
1979–80	0.9	0.9	0.8
1980–81	−1.8	−5.3	−3.7
1981–82	2.2	6.8	3.5
1982–83	2.4	6.3	4.0
1983–84	4.7	8.6	3.9
1984–85	5.5	4.7	1.2
1985–86	8.1	1.8	2.8
1986–87	8.3	4.7	3.6
1987–88	6.8	7.5	4.4

Table B Current-cost operating profit of the nationalized industries

	£ million
1983–84	−183
1984–85	−4030*
1985–86	444
1986–87	318
1987–88	243
1988–89 (estimate)	1837

* This figure was affected by the miners' strike

1. (a) What conclusions, if any, is it possible to derive from the productivity figures in the first table about the performance of the nationalized industries between 1978/79 and 1987/88?
   (b) Do the figures in the second table, showing the operating profit of the nationalized industries, provide evidence of an improvement in the performance of these industries?
   (c) What other information might be useful in assessing the performance of the nationalized industries?
2. How does the size of its 'external financing limit' affect a nationalized industry?
3. To what extent does the data support the view that nationalized industries should *not* be privatized?

Chapter Four

Privatization in theory

'*Privatization is seen as a way of reasserting consumer sovereignty, raising standards of provision, of increasing efficiency and of reducing costs.*' J. R. Shackleton

Denationalization, deregulation and franchising are all methods of privatization (see Figure 1, p. 7), although D. R. Pendse claims that:

'*Any process that reduces involvement of the state or the public sector in a nation's activities, is, in my view, a privatization.*'

Reducing state involvement did not take place until the 1980s. For the three decades preceding, Conservative governments had acquiesced in the retention of the nationalized industries in the public sector; the economic reasons for nationalization went unchallenged. Not until

Mrs Thatcher came to power, in 1979, did traditional Conservatism disappear, to be replaced by *radical market liberalism.*

Much of the credit for this transformation is due to the influence of the work of Professor **Hayek,** a name surprisingly absent from A and AS level textbooks. These texts always include Adam Smith's famous dicta, occasionally in full:

> *'Each individual is led by an invisible hand to promote an end which was no part of his intention. It is not from the benevolence of the butcher, the brewer and the baker we expect our dinner.'*

IN PRAISE OF HAYEK

Like Maynard Keynes, Friedrich von Hayek achieved fame less for what he wrote than for what others said he wrote. The economic philosophy he developed over six decades, and especially during the 20 years he spent at the London School of Economics after 1931, was not, as so many now suppose, 'neo-conservatism'.

Call him instead an original thinker in the tradition of classical liberalism – perhaps the century's finest.

Much of Hayek's work is difficult; all of it is idiosyncratic. His writings seem especially peculiar to economists trained in the modern Anglo-American way, because Hayek rejected that school's paradigm: the idea of a static system in which certain stable properties (many buyers, many sellers, perfect information, homogeneous goods) yield certain stable results (an optimal allocation of resources). Hayek was interested in markets and economies as systems in flux. In his scheme, sequences of events, not states of affairs, were the object of study. Anglo-American economics starts by abstracting from change and time – and is then obliged to reintroduce them, with difficulty, to make its analysis more informative. Hayek, and others of the so-called Austrian school, put change and time at the centre from the outset.

Other themes seem to follow naturally from that perspective. They recur in almost everything Hayek wrote.

The most crucial is the notion of a market as a process of discovery. Modern economies are vastly complicated. Somehow they must process immense quantities of information – concerning the tastes and incomes of consumers, the outputs and costs of production, and the myriad interdependencies of all of the above. The task of gathering this information, let alone making sense of it, is beyond any designing intelligence. But it is not beyond the market, which yields '*spontaneous order*' out of chaos. Hayek looked on the miracle of the invisible hand with the same delight as Adam Smith. He celebrated it anew, and made it his mission to understand it.

Source: abridged from an obituary in *The Economist*, 28 March 1992

So there is a case to be made for adding Hayek's quotable two-word (see the box) 'spontaneous order' to Smith's pithy cliché to form:

the invisible hand gives spontaneous order.

Mrs Thatcher expressed her Hayekian economic philosophy as wanting

'to roll back the frontier of the public sector'.

To accomplish this would require Prime Cuts as drawn by cartoonist Richard Willson. The Chancellor of the Exchequer is about to take a knife to what we have studied:

- defence – the peace dividend
- the NHS market

as well as what is now relevant:

- public sector housing, a pillar of the Welfare State
- railways
- local authorities
- the civil service.

That is, *privatization.*

The benefits of privatization

None of the standard arguments for nationalization can be regarded as incontrovertible.

- *Natural monopolies* can be in the private sector, as they are in the USA. Consumer interests are protected by a regulatory body.
- *Externalities* can be dealt with through recourse to the law, the use of subsidies or the imposition of taxes ('Pigouvian taxes').
- *Income redistribution* is achieved more efficiently through direct income transfer, using transfer payments. Under-pricing national-ized industry outputs is a crude mechanism which is unselective in its impact. It also misallocates resources. There is no obvious size for the public sector. Many of the nationalized industries are the outcome of political zeal, rather than dispassionate economics. With a higher standard of living much the same now can be argued about the Welfare State – a Universal Provider State is by no means necessary, a more efficient **targeting** system is required.

Privatization benefits are considered to be fourfold – two major and two minor. We shall look at the major ones first.

- First, political interference prevents the achievement of *target rates of return*. A privatized sector is a more independent sector.

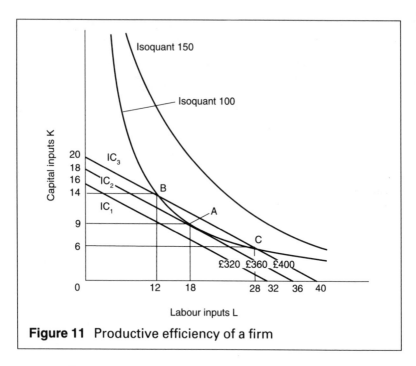

Figure 11 Productive efficiency of a firm

- Secondly, state monopolies create *inefficiency*, are poor in innovation and restrict consumer choice; instead of the consumer being sovereign, power has been transferred to the state and its bureaucracies. Privatization has the potential – depending upon the form it takes – for *widening consumer choice*, giving a better quality of service, lower prices and, for the whole of society, a better, *more efficient use of its resources.*

For economists there are two aspects to efficiency. **Allocative efficiency** occurs when price equals marginal cost. In such circumstances the sovereign with the power is the consumer. Resources are allocated in accordance with changes in consumer preferences and society's resources are at optimal use. For product prices to reflect the cost of provision, barriers to entry and exit of firms should not exist. Contestable markets are essential.

Productive efficiency occurs when a firm minimizes the cost of a given level of output. A profit maximizer automatically seeks productive efficiency. This concept is best illustrated with isoquants and isocosts, as in Figure 11.

An **isoquant** is an equal-output curve. It indicates the combinations of two factor inputs, say capital (K) and labour (L), which can, with given technology, produce a stated output. It is non-linear because one factor is not a perfect substitute for the other. The marginal rate of substitution changes one for the other – if the aim is to maintain a stated output then the slope of the isoquant changes with their ratios.

An **isocost** line is a firm's budget line. Its shape is derived from the relative prices of the factors of production. In Figure 11, capital is priced at £20 per unit and labour at £10 per unit, so isocost IC_1 is plotted at 16 (= £320) on the y-axis and 32 (= £320) on the x-axis. If the aim is to produce output 100, then IC_1 at £320 spends too little to reach it. At B the capital required is 14 (= £280) and labour 12 (= £120), so the cost of 100 outputs is £400. Check 6K and 28L at C to confirm that this is so. A is productively efficient because the price, with 9K and 18L, is reduced to £360.

● There are two further, minor, privatization benefits. First there is *wider shareholding*. The well-publicized sale of familiar state assets, at prices which are attractive to Everyman, can reverse a trend that has been causing concern. The small percentage of the populace owning shares (equities) directly had become so small that commentators had regarded this trend as a weakness of capitalism. At its most simplistic a wider share-owning democracy could be a pro-capitalist democracy. This is, incidentally, hardly an argument for privatization, as such. A post-Communist country establishing capitalism could *give* shares to the public.

● The second minor benefit concerns the *public sector borrowing requirement* (**PSBR**). This is the sum which, each year, central government has to fund for itself, the local authorities and the nationalized industries if they need to borrow because expenditure is greater than income. Asset sales of the 'family silver' reduce the need to borrow. After privatization, any financial capital required by a former state sector enterprise – for new capital investment in factory capacity or plant and machinery – will have to be raised on the private market and will no longer be supplied by the Treasury. Moreover, if each year there are profit taxes from the privatized firms then that year's PSBR can be lower too.

Neither of these subsidiary gains could be used to *justify* privatization; they are merely bonuses.

Criteria for privatization

Lest it now be thought that 'Privatization is Good' and 'State provision is Bad', pause for a moment and reflect on the concept of public goods

– which the state provides and produces because the market would under-produce.

For goods and services which are both rival and excludable, let us introduce the word *pragmatism*. This approach is used in the UK by the Monopolies and Mergers Commission. *It scrutinizes a case on its merits: there are no hard and fast rules.*

The criteria to justify privatization are such that pragmatism becomes the deciding factor: look at each case on its merits and seek out the **aggregate net benefits** to the consumer, both directly and indirectly. Beesley and Littlechild (consult the reading list) mention the following:

- lower prices
- greater output
- better quality and variety
- greater innovation
- changes in the distribution of benefits
- effects on employees, suppliers, exporters and taxpayers.

They write:

> '*Privatization will generate benefits for consumers because privately-owned companies have a greater incentive to produce goods and services in the quantity and variety which consumers prefer.*'

The consumer gains can be summarized as improved allocative and productive efficiency. Privatized entrepreneurs would be motivated to strive for productive efficiency.

'*Competition*', according to Beesley and Littlechild, '*is the most important mechanism for maximizing consumer benefits.*'

It follows, therefore, that statutory barriers to entry, put there by Acts of Parliament, should be removed: **deregulation** is essential.

It may be thought necessary to impose on some privatized industries non-commercial obligations – a rural post office, rural telephone kiosks, some railway lines cannot be expected to pay to cover their private costs of production but confer social benefits to justify their retention. The private benefits measured by the price mechanism under-record their value. Rather than expect **cross-subsidization** whereby one group of consumers pays higher prices to subsidize socially sanctioned outputs, explicit, specific, subsidies from the taxpayer could be negotiated prior to privatization. This is another example of targeting; economic efficiency is increased.

In Figure 12 a privatized monopolist has franchised a rural railway service attracted by the opportunity of normal profit. The monopolist

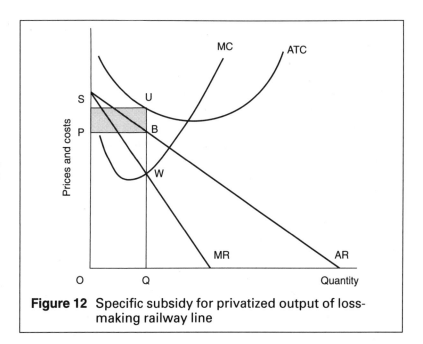

Figure 12 Specific subsidy for privatized output of loss-making railway line

can raise only OPBQ revenue from the passengers, which appears to be, at first, *loss-minimizing* with output OQ passenger miles because marginal cost, MC, is equal to marginal revenue, MR, at W. However, the pre-privatization negotiated subsidy of SUBP, from taxpayers, via the Treasury, added to the commercial revenue from passengers, covers all costs, including opportunity cost. Without the subsidy a loss-making monopolist would not have remained as an operator. Holding a franchise for operation instead of having to buy the rolling stock and line/stations/signals network makes this market contestable: there is no **barrier to exit**.

Privatization and contestable markets

The theory of **contestable markets** has now reached a stage when its already well-established conclusions demand widespread A level attention. Contestability, in the average textbook, is poorly served; yet, for some of the natural monopolies, privatization and contestability seem inseparable.

A perfectly contestable market has no barrier to entry nor to exit: a perfectly competitive market is a contestable market. Not all contestable markets are perfectly competitive markets, however: both oligopolistic and, indeed, pure monopoly markets could be contestable.

The number of firms is irrelevant; the key is the force of potential competition, which, even with profit-maximizing firms, will produce an outcome of only normal profit.

Textbooks always cite the airline industry as being contestable. If a normal profit is not possible on route A then use the same aircraft to fly route B instead. But a recent article by Romer (see the reading list) reveals that managers in the USA have been using Chapter 11 of the Federal Bankruptcy Code to lock in: '*There have been thousands of lay-offs of airline workers, while huge salaries have continued to be drawn by incompetent executives courtesy of the almost permanent haven of Chapter 11.*'

In the context of privatization, a contestable market could be a natural monopoly with its benefit of economies of scale but without the disbenefit of private sector monopoly profit.

The theory of contestability is summarized in Table 3. You will be familiar with the characteristics of both perfect competition and monopoly. Check these against a contestable market.

A natural monopoly may require a huge network of fixed capital, either nationally or regionally. This is so for gas, water, electricity, the postal service's letter-boxes, offices and vans, the telephone lines and exchanges for telecommunications, British Rail's stations, railway track network and rolling stock. These are the nation's **infrastructure**.

This capital represents a huge **sunk cost**: it is capital without an alternative use which is financially not recoverable. Sunk costs are historical costs that cannot be recovered were a firm to leave an industry. The private monopolist firm that has huge sunk costs is locked into an

Table 3 Basic characteristics of perfectly competitive, monopoly and perfectly contestable markets

	Perfectly competitive	Monopoly	Contestable
Number of firms	Large	One	Irrelevant
Size of firms	Small	Substantial	Irrelevant
Barriers to entry/exit	None	Extensive	None
Product of firms	Homogeneous	Homogeneous	May be diversified
Profit levels	Normal profits	Monopoly rents	Normal profits
Managerial motivations	Profit maximization	Profit maximization	Profit maximization

industry, so it has a barrier to exit if the monopolist cannot run it profitably. Simultaneously this barrier to exit is a barrier to entry to a potential entrant: too costly to get in, too costly to get out.

If, when privatizing, the government retained this sunk-cost capital network in public ownership, then it could offer a time-limit **franchise** to a monopolist entrant based on competitive tender. Failure to make a normal profit after say, five years, would be an inducement for it to leave the industry and be replaced by a new, enfranchised entrant. In this contestable market the successful incumbent monopolist would still only make a normal profit – to make excess profit would attract rivals at franchise renewal.

Alternatively, a natural-monopoly common-carrier network could be privatized but regulated. The regulator would supervise the prices charged to the independent firms wishing to use the network. Not having to bear sunk costs means that there would be neither entry nor exit barriers, it would be contestable, e.g. petroleum companies supplying natural gas to the gas grid.

Privatization and the Welfare State

Market failure is the basis of public provision and public production, where needed, of Welfare State goods and services. Neither efficiency in production nor fairness in distribution would be the outcome of a *laissez faire* private market. A Welfare State produces positive externality gains of a healthier, more productive, literate, more caring, better educated citizenry. Equal treatment in health and education is more equitable.

Contemporary critics argue that a Welfare State produces monopolies – the NHS and local catchment-area schools – that merely replace one market failure with another. Large bureaucracies are needed to run these and they are productively inefficient. There is not consumer sovereignty but producer sovereignty.

Privatization proposals could include:

- selling off council houses
- replacing student grants with loans
- the introduction of voucher schemes for school education.

Under the latter, families would 'buy' education at, say, nursery schools of their choice, whether state-run or private, their entitlement to vouchers being a function of income. The government would redeem the vouchers from the schools, for cash. This would be public provision with either public or private production. Student loans would be private provision with public production.

We have studied the internal markets introduced for health and

education. These are not examples of privatization because public provision and public production remain. However, franchising hospital meals and laundry to private producers most certainly is privatization.

It is *not* necessary to 'sell the family silver' when franchising can produce the desired result.

Finally, look carefully at the cartoon. You met its companion in Chapter 2 when the question asked was 'Is profit next to ungodliness?'. There we saw that, to some left-wing ideologists, this was clearly their belief and it motivated their support for nationalization. In this cartoon we now have an alternative view. The angelic entrepreneur no longer has a troubled brow. In a privatized firm he is providing the loaves and fishes that consumers are prepared to pay for in a deregulated, Hayekian market of 'spontaneous order'.

'Privatization is seen as a way of reasserting consumer sovereignty, raising standards of provision, of increasing efficiency and reducing costs.' (J. R. Shackleton)

This is especially so if based on competition.

'Competition is the most important mechanism for maximizing consumer benefits.' (Beesley and Littlechild)

```
                          KEY WORDS

    Hayek                        Aggregate net benefits
    Targeting                    Deregulation
    Allocative efficiency        Cross-subsidization
    Productive efficiency        Contestable markets
    Isoquant                     Infrastructure
    Isocost                      Sunk cost
    PSBR                         Franchise
```

Reading list

Beesley and Littlechild, 'Privatization: principles, problems and regulation' in Kay, Mayer and Thompson, *Privatization and Regulation*, Oxford University Press, 1986.

Romer, S., 'Barriers to exit', *Journal of the Economics and Business Education Association,* winter 1993.

Whynes, D., Chapter 3 in *Welfare State Economics,* Heinemann Educational, 1992.

Essay topics

1. 'Privatizing a nationalized monopoly can increase efficiency only if it is broken up into competitive units.' Discuss. (University of Oxford Delegacy of Local Examinations 1990)

2. Distinguish between consumer sovereignty and producer sovereignty. Discuss whether consumer sovereignty is increased or reduced by (i) advertising, (ii) the privatization of nationalized industries. (Associated Examining Board, 1990)

3. (a) What arguments have been put forward for the privatization of state owned companies? [50 marks]
   (b) To what extent do you feel that experience in the UK has justified the decision to move firms into the private sector? [50 marks]
   (University of London Examinations and Assessment Council 1994)

4. Explain how, in theory, price competition affects the economic efficiency of organizations. What basis is there for the view that government policies on internal markets and privatization are likely to be effective in promoting greater economic efficiency in areas such as education, health and rail transport? (Northern Examinations and Assessment Board 1994)

Data Response Question 4

Passenger transport

This task is based on a question set by the University of Oxford Delegacy of Local Examinations in 1993. Study the tables below and, using your knowledge of economics, answer the questions which follow.

Table A Use and prices

	1981	1986	1988	1989
Use: billion passenger kilometres travelled by:				
Rail	34	37	41	41
Buses and coaches	42	41	41	40
Cars, taxis, and two-wheeled motor vehicles	409	470	526	563
Totals	485	548	608	644
Retail price indices (Jan 1987 = 100)				
Bus and coach fares	69	98	111	119
Rail fares	69	96	108	117
Motoring expenditure	82	98	108	114
Retail prices (all items)	75	98	107	115

Table B Transport, expenditure (£ per week at 1985 prices) and income

	1981	1984	1986	1989
Consumer expenditure per head on:				
Net purchase of motor vehicles, spares and accessories	2.86	3.34	3.82	4.83
Maintenance and running costs of motor vehicles	4.36	4.81	5.24	6.26
Railway fares	0.46	0.49	0.52	0.55
Bus and coach fares	0.69	0.65	0.62	0.61
Expenditure on transport and vehicles as a *percentage* of total consumers' expenditure	14.6	15.1	15.3	16.2
Real household disposable income per head (index numbers 1985 = 100)	92	96	106	123

Source: adapted from *Social Trends 21*, 1991. Crown Copyright. Reproduced by permission of the Controller of Her Majesty's Stationery Office

1. (a) Compare the changes in the use of public transport (rail, bus and coach) with the changes in the use of private transport (cars, taxis and two-wheeled vehicles). [2 marks]

   (b) Describe the changes in public transport use as a percentage of total transport use. [1 mark]

2. (a) Use the data for 1981 and 1989 in Table A to compare the changes in the prices of public transport, motoring expenditure and the retail price index. [2 marks]

   (b) What would happen to the quantity demanded of a product if its price relative to that of other goods changes? [2 marks]

   (c) To what extent do the data in Table A support the theoretical predictions you gave as an answer to (b) above? Comment on your findings. [5 marks]

3. (a) What is meant by the term 'real household disposable income per head'? [2 marks]

   (b) Using the data in Table B, how does expenditure on public and private transport appear to vary with changes in real household disposable income per head? What does this suggest about the economic nature of these two 'goods'? [5 marks]

4. Suggest policy options to deal with the threat of increased road congestion. Where possible use the information given in Tables A and B to support your argument. [6 marks]

Chapter Five

Privatization in practice

'Competition and private ownership are the most powerful engines of economic efficiency and choice. They lead to the creation of world-class companies.' Conservative party manifesto, 1992

The first phase of privatization – the sale of state assets – is now almost at an end. There is little silver left in the cupboard, except Nuclear Electric and the Post Office. Over the last 15 years privatization has moved one million workers and over 50 firms into the private sector, by means of:

- stock market flotations
- trade sales, and
- management buyouts.

The list reads: aerospace, air travel, bus travel, coal, electricity, gas, motor vehicles, railways, steel, shipbuilding, telecoms, water.

For the government the sales have raised over £55 billion. Without this revenue, one or more of the following would have happened:

- taxes would have been higher
- public expenditure would have been lower
- public sector borrowing would have been higher.

Refer to Figure 13 and note the stream of revenue declining.

The government has also aimed for and achieved wider *share ownership*. This is a subsidiary aspect and a political one at that. The number of shareholders in the country has increased from 7 per cent to 25 per cent.

Various criticisms have been directed at the flotations:

- The assets were deliberately under-priced to make them popular. Some flotations were over-subscribed many times. Thus the Exchequer was short-changed to 'bribe' the public.
- The publicity campaigns mounted to persuade investors were intense and consequently very costly. Millions of pounds went to advertising agents in fees as well as to the merchant banks responsible for the flotations. City help does not come cheap.
- Those who bought the shares made handsome profits, either from

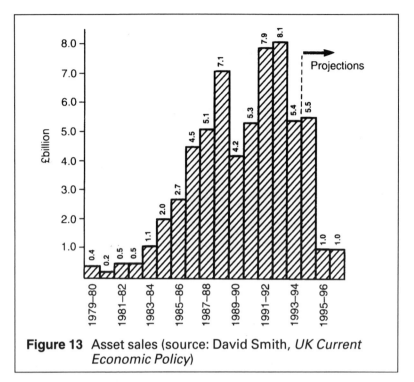

Figure 13 Asset sales (source: David Smith, *UK Current Economic Policy*)

stagging – selling immediately for a capital gain – or through dividends. The monopoly utilities in particular have made handsome profits which have been passed on to shareholders.

In discussing the denationalized firms it is helpful to divide them into two blocks, as in Figure 14. With over 50 to choose from, a knowledge of these will stand an exam candidate in good stead. Note that the left is the *public sector* from which the firms originate as they move to the right, to the *private sector*.

The upper half of the figure has monopolies. If their arrows are horizontal they became privatized monopolies, such as *British Gas*, the 12 *regional electricity boards* (RECS) and the 10 *regional water boards*. The three sloping arrows denote attempts to break up monopolies: *National Power* and *Power Gen* were created as a new duopoly. *British Rail*, which will feature in the next chapter, is an interesting attempt to create a contestable market, through franchising.

We can start in the lower half of the figure where public sector firms faced competition before their transfers. These were uncontroversial privatizations because the continuance of these firms in the public sector would have been hard to justify.

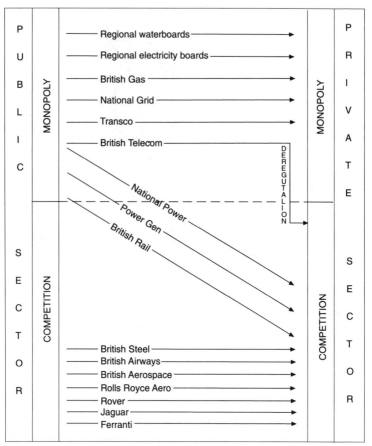

Figure 14 The essential privatizations (adapted from an original idea by David Parker)

Competitive firms

British Airways, freed to set its own targets, has become a global airline which has cut its costs per passenger kilometre to half those of the state-owned Lufthansa. Foreign governments are now copying and pushing their airlines towards privatization.

British Steel, through a single-minded programme of plant closures and enormous job losses, has turned itself into the most efficient steel maker in Europe.

Rolls Royce aero operates in a highly competitive, capital-intensive industry. It is the smallest of the major world firms in its field and financially the weakest in an industry which requires heavy expenditure on research and development. The recession of the early 1990s led to cancelled orders from airlines and the peace dividend has forced a severe cost-cutting programme. The £60 million profit for 1993, on a turnover of £3.5 billion, is less than a building society can expect. This is despite **downsizing**, as businesses call job losses, of 4000 each year. Raising productive efficiency is, of course, what privatization is supposed to be about.

Rover cars and *British Aerospace* are each featured in display boxes, and *Ferranti* is a special case reserved for Chapter 7.

ROVER CARS

Setting behind it the bad taste of the £38 million illegal subsidy the government tried unsuccessfully to conceal in 1989, as well as the absurd giveaway price, Rover has emerged from a transformation which has not gained it, as yet, the recognition it deserves. In an industry that has over-capacity worldwide, it was the only company to increase sales in the recession of 1993.

Rover has emerged from a 1970s nightmare of recurrent, senseless strikes as the state-owned British Leyland conglomerate, which went bankrupt and had to be rescued – so the government of the time argued – with billions of pounds of taxpayers' money.

In the new climate of industrial relations which reforms of the trade unions created in the 1980s, Rover emerged as a testament to the value of those reforms. It started as a classic 'English disease' company – over-manned, with low production, a poor-quality 'lame duck' sheltered from the realities of the market place by successive governments.

Some of the pressure for improvement came from Honda of Japan with which Rover entered into a **joint venture**, sharing research and engine parts. This influence, plus the mainland competition from Japanese implant factories, Nissan and Toyota, has forced the pace of reform. Japanese working practices, with high levels of productivity from workforce flexibility, have replaced the British-style demarcation lines which unions used to use to protect jobs.

Loss-making *Jaguar* was sold off as a *trade sale* to Ford of USA.

Now that BAe has sold off Rover to BMW of Germany, the future of Rover will be watched with close interest. *Can a former state-owned 'lame-duck' which became a golden goose for BAe turn into an executive swan?*

BRITISH AEROSPACE

When set free of state control in 1980, BAe was living in a cosy world of Cold War confrontation, which meant regular orders from the Ministry of Defence. Its civil aviation arm, however, was in a highly competitive world dominated by Boeing.

In the 1980s, BAe consolidated and then proceeded systematically to exploit its new freedom. The government and the taxpayers were the losers.

In 1987 the Royal Ordnance factories, a state monopoly supplier of ammunition to UK armed forces, were sold for only £190 million, as a bargain trade sale to a grateful BAe. A **trade sale** is when one company buys another, direct, without recourse to intermediate shareholders. As the government was the only shareholder, trade sales have been used to privatize:

- Royal Ordnance
- Jaguar motorcars
- Girobank
- Harland and Wolff shipyard
- Rover cars.

Having ruthlessly asset-stripped the capital value of Royal Ordnance by rationalization of plant and by redundancies, BAe used its profits to acquire Rover cars, in 1989, for a nominal £150 million. In fact a 'murky' tax-break 'sweetener' was dangled by the government as an inducement. This was revealed in an investigative article in the *Sunday Times* with the title *'Going for a song'*, which said:

'... the British government goes on trial ... accused of selling the Rover group at a giveaway price.'

Completely unrepentant, BAe promptly sold off Rover's 40 per cent holding in *Daf* of Holland, thus again recouping its purchase price.

However, the Competition Commissioner of the EU ordered repayment of the £38 million sweetener back to the Treasury. This is one of the rare examples to be found of an activity by this Brussels body that impinges on the UK.

Things turned sour in the 1990s with the peace dividend and the recession. With a record loss of £1.2 billion in 1992, BAe was brought to the verge of bankruptcy. It has axed two-thirds of its workforce and closed factories. Currently valued on the market at £2.5 billion, it has long been regarded as a possible takeover victim. Selling Rover to BMW in 1994 eased its cash-flow problems – temporarily.

Regulated utilities

Anxiety over the potential of the utilities – telecommunications, gas, water and electricity – to achieve monopoly profit (refer back to Figure 4, page 19) has led to the establishment of **regulation**. According to the *Penguin Dictionary of Economics*,

> **Regulation is** *'the supervision and control of the economic activities of private enterprise by government in the interests of economic efficiency, fairness, health and safety.'*

Governments create laws, rules and regulations. Governments forbid economic bads such as hard drugs. The Office of Fair Trading and the

Regulators: Stephen Littlechild, Sir Bryan Carsberg and Sir James McKinnon

Monopolies and Mergers Commission are regulatory agencies to see that competition policy legislation is upheld. In addition, privatization has created the need for Directors General of:

- **OFTEL**   –   telecoms
- **OFGAS**   –   gas
- **OFWAT**   –   water
- **OFFER**   –   electricity

They are independent of both government and the utilities. Their Directors General (the cartoon on the previous page shows three) have a lot of power which they use to:

- control prices – this is a conduct issue
- promote competition – this is a structural issue.

The problem the regulators face is that of a common-carrier natural-monopoly network; see again the discussion of Figure 3 (p. 18). Their aim is for **interconnection**; that is, access to competitors who are new entrants. There is a difficulty in establishing equitable and efficient prices for interconnection, but as Professor Martin Cave, employed as a consultant by one of the regulators, has observed:

'It is impossible to get it absolutely right, but not that hard to get it approximately right.'

For the DG of OFWAT this is not even to be attempted. Each of the water boards has a regional monopoly. This regulator therefore has to resort to **yardstick competition** – using comparisons between boards to create an average to use as a measuring rod.

In case the job of the regulator is beginning to look straightforward, let us ponder some pricing/conduct problems first encountered in Chapter 2.

Consider Figure 15. Utilities have a **peak load problem**; demand for telephones, gas and electricity surges at certain times of the day. A monopolist can separate the markets and practise **price discrimination**.

- In the Peak Market shown in (a), users pay the high price P_a. The lower price P_b, in the Offpeak Market shown in (b), attracts OQ_b demand, which, were it to transfer to the Peak Market at the lower price P_b, would overwhelm the network and require more capital capacity to come on-stream. The MC of an extra user, Offpeak, is probably zero, whereas the MC of an extra user, at Peak, is probably an extra power station. Does the regulator have a problem? The output in both markets is where MC equals MR, at W, so the price discriminating monopolist is profit-maximizing.

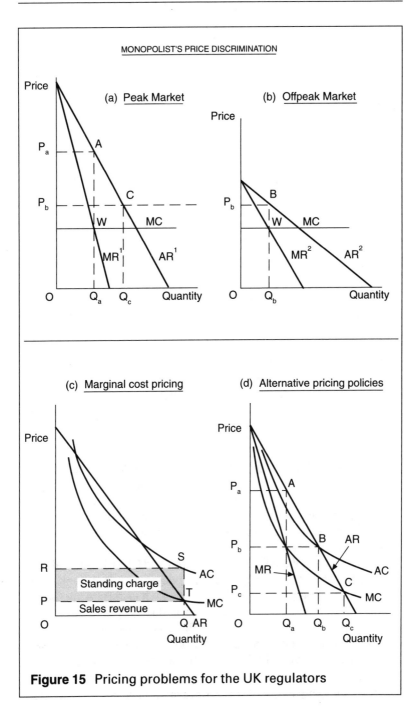

Figure 15 Pricing problems for the UK regulators

- In (c), the utility could use marginal cost pricing as shown in Chapter 2 (Figure 6), but this led to losses. Losses need not result if the utility convinces the regulator that a standing charge is justified – PRST in total from all users – which covers the costs of supply and maintenance of the distribution network.
- Finally, (d) proposes three possible price levels – P_a, P_b or P_c – for you to consider. Which should the regulator allow? If congestion causes confusion, these appear as separate diagrams in Chapter 2.

Regulators and structural reform

According to the 'godfather of privatization', Professor Beesley,

> '*It may be that when full competition does develop, the regulators will be wise enough to immolate themselves.*'

If you have looked up 'immolate' do not take this literally – two of the four regulators are his former pupils and disciples.

As disciples, the regulators have not been content to supervise and alter the price cap; they have pursued an energetic policy of promoting competition. It is to this we now turn in reviewing the activity of the regulatory bodies.

PRICE CAPPING

Price capping is the use of the formula

$$RPI - x$$

where RPI is the *retail price index* familiar to the public for measuring inflation for the average consumer. The percentage figure x is set initially by the government in the industry's privatization legislation. It can be altered subsequently, at the regulator's discretion, to pressurize the firm towards greater *productive efficiency*.

For example, if the RPI is 2.5 per cent and OFTEL sets x at 7.5 per cent, this means BT must *cut* prices by 5 per cent. The outcome will be to squeeze BT's profit, so it is in BT's interests, and that of its shareholders, to improve efficiency to raise profits.

The price cap was an idea of Professor Stephen Littlechild when he was an economics professor at Birmingham University. He is now DG of OFFER and is the 'top dog' on the left in the cartoon on page 57.

● OFTEL

Set up in 1984 as the first regulatory body for a privatized utility, it had to oversee the birth of *Mercury Communications* as the first entrant to face the Goliath, incumbent monopolist, BT. Mercury is a good example of a domestic **infant industry** which did not make a profit until 1992. It now takes 3 per cent of BTs market share away, every year. It already holds 50 per cent of the lucrative City market and 20 per cent of international calls. This looks suspiciously like **cherry-picking** – choosing only the most profitable high-volume customers – the more so now that it is to withdraw its public telephone boxes on the high streets.

In response to this competition BT has cut its labour force by 90 000 since 1984. In real terms, prices have fallen by one-third in that period. The regulator, mindful of excessive profits, including £3 billion in 1990, has raised the x factor in the price cap from 3 to 7.5 per cent. BT has had to cut prices.

In responding to the raising of the x factor, BT has lowered costs and moved into world markets to export its expertise. It is now a world-class company.

The regulator has waived access charges for new entrants needing interconnection to the BT network. *He has completely deregulated the market.* There are no barriers to entry; 33 new telecom firms are already licensed. Look out for *Energis,* owned jointly by National Electric Grid Co. and Lloyds bank – slogan: 'Dial on a Pylon'. Cable TV firms from the USA will further erode BT's market share.

According to the OFTEL regulator:

> '*My test of whether we are getting there is what proportion of customers have a real choice.*'

● OFGAS

According to Clare Spottiswoode, the OFGAS regulator:

> '*The best way to regulate a monopoly is to make it compete.*'

This view, from a Beesley pupil and disciple, illustrates the extent to which regulators have power and are prepared to use it. In the final chapter we shall need to ask: are the regulators out of control?

Backed up by the Monopolies and Mergers Commission – which in 1993 recommended that British Gas should be broken up by restructuring itself internally to separate the network arm (a natural monopoly) from its other activities – the regulator has forced BG to rename its storage and transportation activity *Transco*. Note its position on the 'essential privatizations' chart (Figure 14). The regulator's aim is to make the pipeline *contestable* for the many suppliers now emerging.

The business market has been deregulated and, subject to parliamentary approval, the domestic market will follow. The independents claim they can reduce domestic bills by at least 10 per cent.

Since 1984, BG has reduced its prices, under pressure from the price cap, by 25 per cent in real terms. Having started with 100 000 employees, it will be down to 40 000 by 1996. Like BT it has become a global firm, developing gas supplies and networks in Russia, India and Mexico. They therefore make a useful contribution to the 'invisibles' section of the current account of the balance of payments.

● OFFER

This supervises 12 regional electricity companies, RECs, which supply electricity to customers; also the generators, state-owned Nuclear Electric and the privatized, initially duopolist, generators National Power and Power Gen; and finally the network, National Grid Co. Its DG is Professor Littlechild. Like the OFGAS regulator, he sees his job as

> 'to protect customers and promote competition.'

He has deregulated the generation market. He has ordered the duopolists to put up for sale part of their capacity for new entrants. New entrants – for example some of the RECs and petroleum companies – are, like the duopolists, engaged in building 'new generation' environmentally friendly power stations in what has been dubbed '*the dash for gas*'. Coal power stations can achieve 2.7 pence per kilowatt-hour, nuclear 5.0p and gas 2.2p.

Yet the huge profits made so far, and the enormous share-options awarded to themselves by the directors, have led to a public outcry. The regulator's 1994 review and tightening of the x factor was dismissed as **regulatory capture**. As a monopolist supplier of information, the industry appears to have fed the regulator with just sufficient information to win his approval, so his critics claim (see page 83).

● OFWAT

According to the opinion polls, water privatization was unpopular with four people òut of five. Most were all too aware that each of the ten water boards has a local, geographical monopoly – a natural monopoly – and that if profit, not public service, was to become the name of the water game, then large price rises would ensue.

Even without the privatization of 1989, water charges had to rise to pay for meeting EU water-quality rules, cleaning up our beaches, and coping with environmental concerns over agricultural effluent seeping into our rivers. The treatment of water and sewage have classic elements of both positive and negative externalities. The example of the chemical firm discharging effluent into an adjacent river, using it as a sewer, to the detriment of local bathers, fishermen and ramblers, must be the cliché of economics textbooks. Water is a public health service. It is essential to life. It cannot be provided by competition. Its quality can vary; were this not so, bottled spring water in supermarkets would not be so popular.

OFWAT uses a different formula for price increases. It regulates with:

$$\text{increase} \leq \text{RPI} + k.$$

Your first reaction is to question the plus sign and letter k as printing errors, but k is a positive number to allow increases at a rate *above* inflation. After years of neglect a big investment in new capital is necessary, and this, and a required rate of return, seem to be in conflict with efficiency gains. Incidentally, how does water differ from gas, electricity and telephones when measuring a household's consumption?

Although the RPI has risen 25 per cent since 1989, water boards have averaged price increases of 75 per cent. The monopoly companies have made monopoly profits; their chairmen have quadrupled their salaries and investors have received generous dividends. Evidently public disquiet was justified. The DG's 1994 review reduced the k factor to only 1 per cent above inflation.

Privatizing Britain's housing

A quiet revolution for 1.5 million households has avoided the headlines. For many who lived in *Keir Hardie Terrace*, named after a working-class Labour Party hero, the name has probably changed to *Adam Smith Close*. One of Beveridge's giants, Squalor, has yielded to the 'right-to-buy' legislation for council house tenants, as the boxed extract from the *Economist* explains.

Conclusion

Competition and private ownership have, in some cases, proved to be 'powerful engines of efficiency' for the competitive privatizations – given that competition existed pre-privatization. For the utilities, increasing competition, engineered through deregulation by the regulators, is producing results. It is simply not possible to create competition in water supply. British Airways, British Gas and BT can be regarded as world-class companies. Rolls Royce and BAe are weak. Ferranti International has gone into receivership.

PRIVATIZING BRITAIN'S HOUSING

An Englishman's council home

Barely publicised, little reported, seldom recognised for what it is, it should be the greatest and most significant privatization. In time, it may yet turn out that way – and if it does it will rank as a piece of social engineering with the Labour party's achievements, in the other direction, of 1945–51. But maybe it is as well that only specialists are taking much notice: so far, the government's grand new assault on a century's tradition of state-owned housing is proving a grand old flop.

For those who share its aims, that is all the more disappointing in that the new campaign followed eight years of notable success.

The incoming Tories had an idea of brilliant simplicity: let them buy their council houses. The result was the 'right-to-buy' law of 1980, empowering almost every tenant to buy his home, at a discount that could be large if he had lived there for many years, whether the council liked it or not. The law was an instant and roaring (and vote-winning) success – within two years 350 000 dwellings had been sold – and, with ups and downs, it has been so ever since. By now, sales total 1.25 m, around a fifth of the entire council stock.

Yet that has still left four-fifths – at least £50 billion-worth – in public hands. Inevitably, these are the less desirable residences; in particular, flats in big, ill-designed blocks on big, ill-planned city estates.

Source: *The Economist*, 24 February 1990

KEY WORDS

Stagging	Interconnection
Trade sale	Yardstick competition
Joint venture	Price cap
Downsizing	RPI *minus x*
Regulation	Peak load problem
OFTEL	Price discrimination
OFGAS	Infant industry
OFFER	Cherry-picking
OFWAT	Regulatory capture

Reading list

Anderton, A., Unit A of *The Student's Economy in Focus*, Causeway Press, annually.

Green, R., 'Electricity privatisation, coal and gas', *Economic Review*, Feb. 1994.

Myers, D., 'Privatization of the housing market', *Economic Review*, Nov. 1994.

Swift, S., 'Regulating natural monopolies', *British Economy Survey*, Longman, spring 1993.

Whynes, D., Chapter 7 in *Welfare State Economics*, Heinemann Educational, 1992.

Essay topics

1. Most of the recently privatized companies are regularly reporting large profits. Is this a cause for concern? (Oxford & Cambridge Schools Examination Board 1992)
2. Outline the main economic aims of a programme for the privatization of public assets. In order to achieve these aims, should a government attempt to regulate the behaviour of a privatized undertaking? (Joint Matriculation Board 1992, AS level)
3. (a) Why did the government create regulatory agencies such as OFTEL (for the telecommunications industry) and OFGAS (for the gas industry), when it privatized nationalized industries? [13 marks]
   (b) Discuss the various ways in which such regulatory agencies can influence the performance of these industries. [12 marks] (Associated Examining Board 1993)
4. (a) Explain what you understand by a 'contestable market'.
   (b) Discuss the extent to which contestable markets have become an integral and successful part of the privatization programme in the UK economy since 1979. (University of Cambridge Local Examinations Syndicate 1993, AS level)
5. Privatization has created private monopolies.' 'Privatized monopolies never benefit consumers.' Critically evaluate these statements. (University of London Examinations and Assessment Council 1994)

Data Response Question 5

British Telecom's performance

This task is based on a question set by the Oxford & Cambridge Schools Examination Board in 1991. Read the following extracts from BT reports and the *Sunday Times* and then answer the questions.

We spent the best part of £2.9 billion on progressing the modernisation of our huge telephone network, improving its reliability, adding to its services and extending it to 24 million customer lines. We froze our 'basket' of regulated charges – which includes rental and inland calls – from 1986 for three years, and by June 1989 our prices were 16% below inflation. By May 1989, inflation was 8.3%, putting great pressure on our costs and threatening to affect our investments in network modernisation. We have agreed with OFTEL that we will not put up our main prices overall by more than 4.5% below inflation.

(*BT Report to Customers*, August 1989)

The quality of service to our customers by the end of the financial year was the best that we had ever achieved. We continued our price freeze on main services throughout the year. Clearly there was no way in which we could maintain our price freeze for ever. The modest increases of an average of 3.2% will help us to meet our objective of achieving profitable growth. Despite our achievements, however, we face growing competition in our domestic market. **And that competition is actually promoted by a political and regulatory environment that discriminates positively in favour of new entrants to our domestic market**. We look forward to the day when competition is fair, to the day when regulatory discrimination is no longer necessary.

(*BT Report to Shareholders*, September 1989)

BT is planning to increase telephone charges by up to 11.8%. Domestic customers who make the fewest calls will be the hardest hit. The biggest of the rises will be on the cost of renting lines (up from £71 to £79 a year) and on new connection fees (up from £133 to £148). The company was accused last week of exploiting its monopoly on private lines. BT, which made £3 billion profit last year, defended the proposals, which are expected to be rubber-stamped by OFTEL. **It said the increases were part of a drive to make the price of calls more competitive by reducing subsidies.** 'We want our prices to reflect more closely what it costs us to provide the services,' said a spokesman. **Critics argued that BT was shifting the burden on to private subscribers to avoid the risk of alienating commercial customers.**

(*Sunday Times* report, July 1990)

1. Explain the sentences in bold type.
2. What conclusions can be drawn about British Telecom's pricing strategy from the above extracts? Are the proposed price increases justified?
3. What is the rationale behind regulation of British Telecom's activities? Is regulation effective? Is regulation desirable?

Chapter Six

Privatization in the nineties

'Next Steps has created fewer headlines than asset sales or deregulation, but in many ways it represents a more dramatic, if longer term, change' David Smith, UK *Current Economic Policy*

As the above cartoon pinpoints, the denationalization part of the Tory privatization programme is reaching the end of the line. Coal and rail were privatized in 1994. Only the Post Office and Nuclear Electric remain.

Deregulation has started to open up competition in the former state-sector monopolies of gas, electricity and telecoms. The most successful deregulation that the public seems to be aware of is that of buses on long-distance express routes. Prices have tumbled and the quality of the buses has changed up to a new level: 'Refreshments, Hostess Service, Video, Reclining Seats, Toilets'. This is a testament to competition but, as the box overleaf shows, there may be 'corpses on the lawn'.

Competitive franchising (described in the box on page 70) is the privatization of the nineties.

One franchise that has hit the headlines is prison escort duties. Unfortunately *Group 4,* a Dutch security firm, seemed to be making a speciality of letting prisoners escape – according to the clipping from the *Daily Mail* it was producing 'a comedy of errors'.

Setting aside the satire, there is a strong economic case for privatized prisons. The prison service has historically been provided by an inefficient monopoly and might well benefit from the shock of competition. The service seems to be poorly managed. One of the privatized prisons, Blakenhurst, has reduced the weekly cost of looking after a prisoner from £437 to £310.

There is nothing like 'corpses on the lawn' for discouraging new entrants

SIR GORDON BORRIE

When the bus industry was deregulated, it was brought fully within the scope of the general competition legislation and it was not thought necessary to create an OFBUS. Competition was being encouraged from the outset, primarily by privatization and the breaking up of the National Bus Company, and it was thought there was no need for special regulation.

Predictably, the structure proved to be unstable, and there have been many subsequent mergers resulting in some quite large, if geographically spread, new-style operators. Several mergers have been referred on my advice to the MMC and divestment ordered following adverse reports from the MMC, but challenge in the courts has made the future of this application of competition policy uncertain.

Further, the established local operators have exploited the many advantages they have over potential, usually small-scale, entrants, which advantages reduce in practice the *contestability* of the bus market.

One advantage is control of an essential facility, such as a bus station. It is an anomaly, perhaps, that whereas the 1985 Act required that the operator of a publicly owned bus station shall make that facility available to all operators on a non-discriminatory basis, there is no such provision for privately owned bus stations. In 1986, acting under the Competition Act 1980, I did rule as anti-competitive the refusal by Southern Vectis, the dominant bus operation on the Isle of Wight, to allow a small competitor to use its bus station at Newport because of the lack of any alternative, reasonably comparable facility. I accepted an undertaking from Southern Vectis to allow competitors access on payment of a non-discriminatory cost-related fee.

Another feature of the bus market since deregulation, which may also be of wider relevance, is *strategic predatory behaviour* – usually the use of predatory prices – designed to eliminate competitors and deter subsequent new entrants. In one writer"s phrase: there is nothing like some 'corpses on the lawn' for discouraging new entry. Up to the end of 1990 we have had 105 complaints of predatory behaviour by established bus operators against (usually small) new entrants.

The dividing line between predatory and aggressive, but wholly legitimate, competitive behaviour is a notoriously difficult one to define and apply and, generally, I believe that competition authorities (and regulators) should err on the side of caution before taking action in response to allegations of predation. But where the market structure and characteristics of the firms involved suggest that predation could well be a profitable strategy in the long-run sense, then intervention may well be justified.

Sir Gordon Borrie was Director General of the Office of Fair Trading
Source: *Economic Affairs,* September 1991

BREAK-OUT NUMBER SEVEN AFTER COMPANY IS WARNED

Another prisoner lost in 'comedy of errors'

ANDREW LOUDON

THE privatised prison escort shambles took another turn for the worse yesterday when Group 4 guards lost another man.

Terence Hyman's dash from Sheffield magistrates court made him the seventh of the company's charges to go free in less than two weeks.

He has just been sentenced to 14 days in jail for non-payment of fines totalling £422. Two Group 4 custody officers were called to the court to take him away but as they arrived he ran for the door.

The guards tried to block his escape and restrain him with handcuffs, but Hyman fought them off and the struggle continued into the street.

One of the guards suffered facial injuries before 29-year-old Hyman, from Gleadless, Sheffield, eventually ran off.

The escape came the day after the head of the prison service, Derek Lewis, exonerated Group 4 from blame over similar problems which marred the first week of the firm's operations. He said he would not impose any penalties on the company.

Mr Lewis admitted, however, that switching 'overnight' to the private service had not been a success and said future contracts would be phased in.

Group 4 is being called back to the prison service in a month to review its performance. Under the five-year contract, worth £9.5 million annually, it delivers all prisoners, except top security Category A inmates, in the Humberside and East Midlands area to court and provides security while they are in the court cells and docks.

The contract can be terminated if the number of prisoners reaching court on time each month drops below 98 per cent.

Group 4 says that not all the escapes have been its fault. Some have arisen from difficulties outside its control.

But Labour home affairs spokesman Tony Blair said last night: 'This comedy of errors must be brought to an end forthwith. It is time for the Home Secretary to get a grip of the prison escort service and ensure public safety.

'If he cannot be satisfied that Group 4 are providing a service in an effective way he must take steps for the contract to be withdrawn.'

Daily Mail, 17 April 1993

The success of the piecemeal franchising of the 1980s has convinced the government that the scope for franchising public sector services is enormous.

Market testing is the essential key. The Local Government Act of 1988 has made it compulsory for all local authorities to put their services out to tender. Covering an annual expenditure of £1.5 billion, the aim is greater efficiency and lower costs through competition.

Next Steps has become the Conservative government's programme to extend compulsory tendering to central government expenditure over the range, value and staff outlined in the box. This takes

COMPETITIVE FRANCHISING

Under competitive franchising, firms compete *for* a market, not *in* a market. The right is achieved through competitive tender. This type of auction relies on competition at the licensing stage to eliminate monopoly prices and practices. The award is on the basis of lowest price with a guarantee of quality. The Press has dubbed it 'semi-privatization'. Examples from the 1980s include refuse collection, hospital meals and laundry, schools meals. All of these are

public sector provision but **private sector production**

NEXT STEPS: GOVERNMENT ACTIVITIES TO BE MARKET-TESTED

- **Information technology**
  Agriculture
  Customs & Excise
  Defence
  Employment
  Foreign Office
  Inland Revenue
  Lord Chancellor
  N. Ireland
  Office of Public Service & Science
  Trade and Industry
  Transport
  Welsh Office

- **Legal services**
  Agriculture
  Customs & Excise
  Environment
  Lord Chancellor
  Social Security

- **Accounting services**
  Customs & Excise
  Environment
  Health
  Home Office
  Lord Chancellor
  N. Ireland
  Office of Public Service & Science
  Scottish Office
  Social Security
  Trade and Industry
  Treasury
  Welsh Office

- **Typing and secretarial services**
  Agriculture
  Customs & Excise
  Employment
  Inland Revenue
  N. Ireland

large-scale privatization from blue-collar operations in local government to white-collar operations in Whitehall. There have been some interesting headlines in the Press. Here is a representative selection:

'Tories to privatize income tax records'
'Air traffic control to be privatized'
'The Army may go to war in leased vehicles'
'Police records, courts, services and census face privatization'
'Private firms tender to build new toll roads'

You may find your school or college being inspected soon. In the past this task would have been done by Her Majesty's Inspectors; now it is in the hands of privatized OFSTED, the Office for Standards in Education.

In a sense the 1994 privatization of British Rail conforms to this theme: the government, having suffered so much criticism from economists for not making the utilities contestable, so that the regulators had to step in and reform them, has tried franchising instead of denationalization. Ownership of track signals and stations has been separated from ownership of trains. Both are available, under contract, to those who bid successfully for a franchise to run services. To break the problem of access to the natural monopoly track, this is run by *Railtrack*. This makes its use contestable; users pay fees to Railtrack. Those who decide not to renew a franchise do not face exit barriers. Rolling stock will be leased from leasing companies. There will be a regulator and a franchise awarder. No wonder the Minister responsible for bringing this to fruition looks under pressure in David Smith's cartoon. Experts think it will take 20 years to complete the restructuring.

Privatizing coal, also in 1994, was more straightforward but not a public flotation. It was a trade sale, by tender, to R. J. B. Mining. There are only 17 pits still in operation, although open-cast mining is very important. The market for British Rail has contracted steadily as car ownership has risen; the market for coal has collapsed dramatically – 50 years ago there were 850 pits. For long, sheltered behind **protectionism** – an embargo on cheaper, imported coal – British Coal was, in the words of a former Chancellor of the Exchequer, Nigel Lawson:

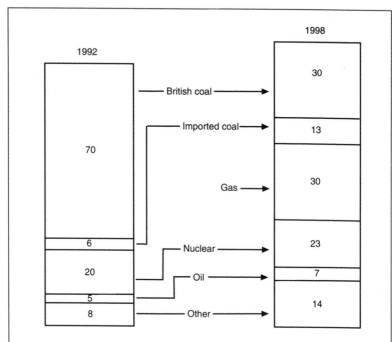

Figure 16 Power station energy sources in England and Wales, in million tonnes coal equivalent (source: *The Economist*)

'...the archetypal public corporation where genuine business management was almost unknown'.

Lifting of the embargo on foreign coal accompanied the privatization of the electricity industry, to make the latter more attractive to shareholders. Figure 16 shows a doubling of coal imports by 1998. More important is the *'dash for gas'* which spells *'dole for coal'*. The demand for coal-fired power stations is collapsing as cheaper gas-fired ones replace them. At the start of the year-long miners' strike in 1984, the leader of the National Union of Miners warned his comrades that if they did not win the fight the industry would be 'butchered'. He was right. Exposing coal to the realities of the market has proved to be agonisingly painful as whole mining communities have been decimated.

KEY WORDS

Competitive franchising	Market testing
Public sector provision	Next Steps
Private sector production	Protectionism

Reading list
Ingham, A., 'Rail privatization: too much or too little?', *Economic Review*, April 1993.

Essay topics
1. Why privatize? Discuss with reference to examples of privatization in the UK economy since 1979. [20 marks] (University of Cambridge Local Examinations Syndicate 1992, AS level)
2. 'We believe that the best way to produce a profound and lasting improvement on the railways is to end British Rail's state monopoly' (Conservative party election manifesto 1992). Discuss. (Oxford & Cambridge Schools Examination Board 1993)
3. Explain the different concepts of efficiency. Evaluate the view that all forms of monopoly violate the requirements for economic efficiency and therefore can never operate in the public interest. (Northern Examinations and Assessment Board 1994)
4. (a) Explain the main economic issues involved in the privatization of British Rail. [12 marks]
   (b) Comment on the extent to which these issues are specific to this particular privatization. [8 marks] (University of Cambridge Local Examinations Syndicate 1994, AS level)

5. In the United Kingdom, refuse collection has traditionally been financed and provided directly by local authorities. More recently, local authorities have been forced to put their refuse collection out to competitive tendering.

(a) In what way does the process of competitive tendering involve a greater use of the price mechanism? [5 marks]

(b) Discuss the possible advantages and disadvantages of making greater use of the price system for the provision of refuse collection. [15 marks] (Associated Examining Board, AS Level, 1994)

Data Response Question 6

Anger erupts at coal pit closures

This task is based on a question set by the Welsh Joint Education Committee in 1993. The data below include an adaptation of an article published in the *Financial Times* on 14 October 1992. Study the data carefully, then answer *each* of the questions which follow.

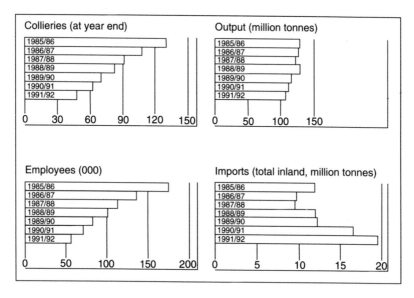

British Coal yesterday announced sweeping cuts in its operations with the shutdown of 31 pits and the loss of 30 000 jobs. Mr Neil Clarke, British Coal's chairman, said the cuts were necessary 'in the light of harsh conditions in the electricity market and the need to bring supply and demand back into balance'. Coal stocks at power stations currently stand at 18 months' supply.

He said it was clear that the company's sales of coal to electricity generators, its main customers, would be sharply reduced next year to 40 million tonnes from 65 million tonnes this year.

Mr Clarke warned that the 'dash for gas', the replacement of coal-fired electricity power stations by gas-fired stations, would push up electricity prices and result in a huge excess of generating capacity. Plans for gas-fired stations would squeeze 30 million tonnes of coal a year out of the market.

British Coal currently sells coal for about 1.5 times the world market price, but its prices are set to fall by 27% after April 1993.

There is some dispute over the relative costs of coal and gas for electricity generation. Gas-fired plants are cheaper to build. Some older coal-fired plants have lower costs than gas, but this is largely due to the 'sunk' costs of construction already written off. Only a small number of pits can produce coal cheaply enough to allow coal-fired power stations to compete on a full-cost basis.

Mr Michael Heseltine, President of the Board of Trade, stated that 'British Coal cannot go on producing coal which cannot be sold'. Pointing to the current level of subsidies for British Coal of £100 million per month, Mr Hestletine argued that 'if you are trying to make British industry competitive, helping to contain its costs with the cheapest power available is essential'.

1. Using the bar charts, explain what happened to British Coal's labour productivity between 1985/86 and 1991/92. [3 marks]
2. How are the changes in the number of collieries and in labour productivity likely to have affected British Coal's costs? [4 marks]
3. Why did British Coal feel that it was essential to close pits? [6 marks]
4. 'There is some dispute over the relative costs of coal and gas for electricity generation.' Explain how the calculation of costs is relevant to this dispute. [6 marks]
5. Discuss the arguments *for* and *against* subsidizing British Coal to continue its current level of production. [6 marks]

Chapter Seven

Privatization and the public sector

'So, you think you've changed, do you?', the caterpillar asked Alice.

Privatize or nationalize?

If challenged as to the appropriate relative sizes of the public and private sectors, traditional economics has no answer. Where the UK should be on the spectrum of *laissez faire* to command economy is a **normative** question; most of us agree that a **mixed economy** is to be preferred, but economists cannot be expected to agree on its boundaries.

Economists can, however, make a very meaningful contribution in the debate over particular cases. Privatization is a **supply side** measure aimed at making markets work better. An economist will look at an industry or firm as a candidate for public sector provision and production if it involves public good externalities, merit externalities or monopoly; the expectation would be that private provision and production would lead to a sub-optimal outcome. State involvement produces Paretian improvements that make some people better off.

The argument for privatization involves a belief in competition because it improves productive and allocative efficiency; a suspicion that public sector bureauracracy causes major resource misallocation; and that wider share-ownership is worthwhile for its own sake and because it underpins capitalism and the 'invisible hand' of the price mechanism.

These are the arguments but they cannot be delivered on tablets of stone because they may apply some of the time, in some of the cases. Deregulation works if it encourages competition; it does not if it allows establishment of an unregulated monopoly. Franchising can work, with the right firm; but not all the franchised firms are the right firms. The safest approach is an analysis of each firm or industry to seek out incontrovertible aggregate net benefits.

Economists have been suspicious of privatizing monopoly utilities. Their importance to the infrastructure is such that they cannot be allowed to go bankrupt. But the priority of their shareholders is profit.

Economic solutions can be found to these problems – greater contestability through franchising or regulatory supervision.

As a general guideline the following microeconomic and macroeconomic aspects of economics are involved in privatization. Whether they justify an individual case is a cause for debate.

Possible microeconomic gains from privatization

● Welfare gains in efficiency

In an economic environment of decision-making for want satisfaction, a *'first best'* solution would be if consumer sovereignty existed in its purest form. The competitive ideal of price equal to marginal cost supposes perfect knowledge, no externalities and perfect factor mobility.

In the economics of the real world the supporters of privatization argue for a *second best* solution as being a realistic aim because achieving it would be a definite improvement on the *third best* inefficiencies of the public sector. What is the evidence?

The gains in allocative efficiency are proved by the fall in prices and rise in quality for long-distance bus travellers and users of gas, electricity and telephones. Greater productive efficiency has been achieved by Jaguar and the National Freight Corporation, by British Aerospace, Rolls Royce and Cable & Wireless. The restructuring at Rover Group was the start of productive efficiency gains which justified the return of Rover to the private sector as a former, wounded hero, rather than 'lame duck'. Its takeover by BMW seems to endorse this view. The utilities are now far more productively efficient. British Steel is held to be an exemplar.

● Investment appraisal and efficiency

A privatized corporation has to borrow in a commercial capital market such as the City or abroad; the Exchequer is relieved of the necessity to produce the funds. The privatized borrower has to conform to the private-sector capital investment criteria which are more stringent than those of the Treasury, however much the Treasury would wish to simulate the market. The factors of production – the nation's resources – are the crucial inputs in the supply equation of firms, which, if misallocated, cause waste, i.e. sub-optimal efficiency. In order to gain public sympathy, privatizing governments stress direct consumer benefits of their programmes; economists seek also the less direct, but equally important, 'hidden' gains. It is easy to see that breaking a monopoly and exposing a corporation to competition – e.g. Mercury Communications challenging BT – is a consumer benefit. Consumers will also gain, however, when BT has to compete in the capital markets for the funds it will require to develop its telecommunications equipment.

- ● **Entrepreneurs and dynamic efficiency**

Freed from the 'dead hand of Whitehall' and the interference of government ministers, entrepreneurs are likely to take the view that privatized firms will operate like the rest of the private sector and so offer the business opportunities that enterprising managers seek along with the rewards – higher incomes, job satisfaction, prestige and power which the public sector cannot produce. If better calibre management is an outcome of privatization, then the productive and allocative efficiency gains hoped for may become a reality.

Consider the *Ferranti factor*. When privatized in 1980, Ferranti International was Scotland's biggest industrial employer with a workforce of 23 000. In 1987 its management was duped into buying a US defence firm for £420 million with contracts 'worth billions of dollars'. Actually these were bogus and Ferranti finally went into receivership in 1993. Not every entrepreneur is a 'frog prince'.

- ● **Natural monopolies and efficiency**

Natural monopolies require *contestable markets* to force down costs; entry and *exit* that is frictionless so the monopolist cost-minimizes.

The common-carrier grids of gas, electricity and of BT are in the private sector. The regulators have had to step in and alter what the government botched:

- ● Henceforth *Transco* will run the gas grid, without any customer final sales, so that all gas supplier entrants to the industry will have no interconnection barriers.
- ● The Director General of OFFER has pressurized the regional electricity companies to divest themselves of their jointly-owned grid and make it an independent *National Grid Co.*
- ● BT has been instructed by OFTEL to give equal access to all new telecom entrants.

The belief of 'The public sector in theory', Chapter 2, was that these natural monopolies were unthinkable in the private sector.

- ● **Trade unions and productive efficiency**

The trade unions feature in the consequences of privatization in relation to the former nationalized industries. The unions have, over the years, established themselves strongly in the public sector where the absence of the profit motive, shareholders, stock market ratings and market pressures have weakened management power in collective bargaining and correspondingly strengthened that of the unions. Large pay claims have been more readily conceded in the public sector, and

'... *the princess was astonished to see, instead of the frog, a hand-some prince.*'

Grimm's Fairy Tales

Unfortunately some entrepreneurs stride forth from the Public Sector Pond to the Private Sector Kingdom, in Chris Riddell's cartoons, with more hope than ability.

restrictive labour practices, which protect overmanning, are strongly entrenched.

Supply-side reforms can be explicit; e.g. the labour market reforms designed to reduce the monopoly power of unions. *Privatization is a supply-side reform by stealth if it also achieves this outcome.*

● Job creation

Direct **job creation** in the privatized sector has been limited: Jaguar recruited an extra 1000 operatives because of the success of its new models. For the most part the firms and industries involved have shed jobs before flotation, under pressure to make a success of their launch. The trade unions in telecommunications opposed privatization fearing that a private-sector British Telecom would be more cost-conscious and efficiency-motivated than a public-sector BT. They were correct. Thus far, privatization seems to have been a recipe for lengthening dole queues. Not so.

More efficient privatized firms create jobs in supplier industries as the privatized firms expand sales. More motor cars made means a rise in demand for headlights, leather upholstery, walnut fascias, etc. More efficient, labour-shedding firms, after privatization, create jobs in other sectors of the economy if they reduce their prices, and these are important inputs for other firms: cheaper gas and telephones means lower costs for British industry. Sacked BT employees have received large redundancy cheques and immediately taken up new jobs with rival telecommunications firms. Privatization becomes the begetter of longer-term *hidden employment* even though it may create *direct unemployment* in the short run. But unemployed ex-miners are a problem.

● Competition policy

Privatization gets a green light when it exposes former public sector activities to competitive market forces. The formal meaning of '**competition policy**' is the legislation from 1948 to 1980 and the investigatory bodies it has created – the Office of Fair Trading, Monopolies and Mergers Commission and the Restrictive Practices Court – which have been instructed to further the public interest by seeking out anti-competitive practices and subjecting enterprises to efficiency audits. Privatization is a form of competition policy.

The creation of OFGAS, OFTEL, OFWAT and OFFER as separate supervisory entities adds to the bodies created by law. These bodies are not without their critics and there have been differences of opinion as to whether the regulators are themselves out of control (see the box).

ARE THE REGULATORS OUT OF CONTROL?

Martin Cave

Regulated industries are scarcely ever out of the news. The summer of 1994 was a key period because, in the course of it, two major reviews were being undertaken which will influence water prices and electricity prices for the rest of the century. The key point is that, in the final analysis, the judgement of a single person in each case – Ian Byatt, Director of Water Services in the case of the water industry and Professor Stephen Littlechild, Director General of Electricity Supply, in the case of the electricity companies – was decisive in formulating the initial proposals. A Director General can have a major impact upon policy.

A few unelected regulators have played a critical role in determining not only the structure but also the conduct of the utilities. The question is: *Are they behaving effectively, in consumers' interests, and does the system satisfy the necessary conditions for accountability in a democracy?*

The first point to make is that industry regulators in fact share their powers to some degree with others. Thus in legal terms, crucial decisions about structure are made by the relevant government minister. This is demonstrated, for example, by the fact that it was Mr Heseltine, the President of the Board of Trade, who had the final say in determining the shape of British Gas. Secondly, regulated companies can appeal to the Monopolies and Mergers Commission on many aspects of decisions taken by the industry regulator. They claim that the costs of doing this are prohibitive, but the opportunity is still there.

One method of making regulators more politically accountable would be to relocate them in government departments rather than as the non-ministerial departments which in current circumstances they are. The problem here is that while accountability would increase, the scope for political interference would increase too. This might make the companies less desirable to invest in, and increase their cost of capital.

So, are they out of control? Or even if they aren't, should better safety nets be introduced to reform the system? My view is that so far regulators have managed to walk the tightrope between the interests of consumers and the interests of investors quite successfully. The high rates of return have certainly been observed but (a) they are now likely to come down sharply, and (b) investors need to be confident of returns if they are to devote their capital to long-term businesses like the utilities. With some exceptions, regulators have been careful to explain the reasoning behind their decisions and to give interested parties an opportunity to make observations on them. So I do not believe that regulators are out of control.

But this does not mean that reforms are unnecessary or undesirable:

- One possibility would be to increase the number of regulators to a panel of, say, five. This would depersonalise the decisions to some extent.
- Secondly, regulators could be made to explain their strategy to the public rather more fully. This would expose them to more public criticism.
- Thirdly, Parliament could set up a special committee to examine conduct of regulation. Every year, say, each regulator would be invited to attend and give an account of his or her strategy and how it had been implemented. Such a procedure would close the loop between Parliament in setting up the regulatory bodies and the accountability of the regulators to Parliament. The regulators would not much like it, and it would not be perfect, but it would be an improvement.

Brunel University, Teachers' Conference, 1994

- ## Wider share ownership
This is a political factor, with economic implications. It is aimed at underpinning capitalism and hoping for right-wing votes at future elections. This is a normative issue.

Macroeconomic aspects of privatization

- ## Fiscal policy
One reason for rolling back the frontier of the public sector has been the belief that it would produce lower taxes on incomes. A supply-side reformer would also point to the incentive effect of lower taxes; a critic would wonder why the 'privatization swag' could not have been put back into state-funded capital projects – new hospitals, schools and prisons, for example.

- ## The public sector borrowing requirement
The **PSBR** is the shortfall of the public sector in receipts compared with expenditure. The large sums raised each year from privatization have been used to either reduce the PSBR, cut taxes or maintain public expenditure at a higher level than it would have been otherwise. Using privatization money in these ways has provoked the criticism of 'subsidizing a riotous living'. This is a further aspect of fiscal policy but is highly contentious.

- ## Crowding out
In so far as the City showed an insatiable appetite for the privatization equity shares, then, when the natural monopolies were marketed, the flow of money into them, was so great that some private sector firms found it difficult to float a rival new issue at the same time. This is **crowding out**.

Firms that turn instead to bank loans increase the money supply. If there are money supply growth targets these are put under pressure and may be breached.

- ## The balance of payments
Some of the demand for shares has come from abroad, on a large scale. The Japanese are said to hold 8 per cent of British Gas shares. The accusation of 'selling the family silver' got a rough ride in Chapter 1; but it is true to say that, as non-residents are not part of the family, dividends paid to them in subsequent years out of profits will constitute a debit outflow item on the *interest, profit and dividends* part of the **invisibles account** (services) of the balance of payments.

Negative aspects of privatization

Until 'Thatcherism' turned sour in the recession of the early 1990s, its motivation in the 1980s had been based on a belief in a property-owning democracy and enterprise culture growing at the expense of a welfare society and dependency. The 'economic miracle' would be engineered by supply-side measures, prominent among then, privatization. Clearly there have been some gains and some losses.

- Selling heavily-discounted council houses has not helped to change the quality of life in the remaining four-fifths of public housing; but buyers who were in a position to afford a mortgage are also now the recipients of a taxpayer-subsidized capital gain. This is a clear redistribution of income which is debatable on equity grounds.
- Rich pickings have also come the way of the army of City firms,

---

COMMENT
Plugged in to greed

THE electicity industry regulator Professor Stephen Littlechild should have his report on reducing prices for consumers thrown straight back at him and be told to come up with a set of proposals which are more realistic.

He is appointed by the Government, paid by the taxpayer and given powers to ensure that electricity users get a fair deal. This is something which he has signally failed to do.

An average saving of £18 a year for a domestic customer is nothing short of pathetic.

It is objectionable for millions who have to struggle to pay their bills while bosses, such as two-day-a-week Bryan Weston of MANWEB, and shareholders rake in eye-popping profits and perks.

Over the past weeks *Today* has been at the forefront in exposing the greed of bankers, water board directors and now those running the electricity industry.

We have shown how targets can be altered to enhance payments to old buffers and others given boardroom seats on the basis of "you scratch my back and I'll scratch yours" to the detriment of the customer and employee.

The report by Professor Littlechild was trailed as a big crackdown on the gross profits of regional electricity companies.

The City's reaction proved beyond doubt that it was anything but. Share prices in the companies shot up. It was seen as a renewal of licences to print money for the top dogs.

Even more sickening are the suggestions that the losses will be offset by cuts in staff over the coming months.

It is time the Government told its servant, Professor Littlechild, to order this particular monopoly to forget about money-grubbing directors and shareholders for a change and put consumers first.

Today, 12 August 1994

merchant banks, brokers and advisers involved in the flotations. The privatization programme has for them meant fat profits.

- In the queues of would-be purchasers of shares, the genuine capitalists were in a minority; the majority were happily grabbing a guaranteed capital gain, offered by an obliging government which seemed to underprice the issues deliberately to ensure that novice 'stags' became richer at the expense of the taxpayers in general. In some cases, the family silver was practically given away – philanthropic asset-stripping, perhaps?
- Not only was the Rover affair unedifying; it also gave professionals the opportunity to asset-strip on a scale which made the original sale look like daylight robbery. The government has now had to insert 'clawback' clauses in privatization legislation so that the taxpayer does not lose if this happens again.
- It is argued that sales of state assets could and should have produced revenue for improving the health service and education – the state of which, according to opinion polls, is causing great public disquiet.
- Profits have been excessive for the utilities. Figure 4 in Chapter 2 correctly forecast the outcome for a privatized monopoly. Only now are the regulators starting to address this problem with further increases in the x factor of the industries' price caps.
- Salaries have provoked a public outcry and even the Archbishop of Canterbury has preached from the pulpit about the greed of managers of privatized firms. Former state managers have been dipping into the honey pot, awarding themselves enormous pay rises and generous share options that have turned some of them into paper millionaires. The leader from the *Today* newspaper (see the clipping) represents the strength of feeling of the general public. The chief executive of British Gas gave himself a 75 per cent pay rise in 1994, and at North West Water after 5 years in the private sector the salary of the chief executive had risen by 571 per cent.

Conclusion

'So, you think you've changed, do you?', the caterpillar asked Alice. Although undoubtedly clever – the daughter of a headteacher, no less – Alice lived at a time (1862) when privatization was unknown so this is one particular riddle she would have found difficult. We shall have to supply her the answer, assuming the caterpillar was referring to privatized firms and industries.

'It all depends,' said Alice.

- 'It depends on whether you take a short-term or long-term view.

- It depends on which type you mean – denationalization, franchising or deregulation.
- It depends on the specific example and whether there are aggregate net benefits in the public interest.
- It depends on whether you ask a chairman of one after he has tried to change from a frog to a prince.'

According to his author, Grimm, the frog said: 'I want not your pearls and jewels.'

KEY WORDS

Normative	Competition policy
Mixed economy	PSBR
Supply side	Crowding out
Job creation	Invisibles account

Reading list

Parker, D., 'Privatization: what do economists think?', *Economics Today*, Anforme, June 1993.

Parker, D., 'Privatization Ten Years On', in Healey, N. (ed.), *Britain's Economic Miracle*, Routledge, 1993.

Smith, D., Chapter 9 in *UK Current Economic Policy*, Heinemann Educational, 1994.

Essay topics

1. In the light of the economic changes that have occurred within the UK in recent years, discuss whether it is still correct to describe the UK economy as a mixed economy. (Associated Examining Board 1990)

2. (a) What were the expected economic benefits of privatization policy in the UK? [40 marks]

(b) Using examples, examine the extent to which these benefits have been realized. [60 marks] (University of London Examinations and Assessment Council 1995)

3. In 1988, the main sources of primary energy in the UK economy were approximately as follows: solids (chiefly coal) 25 per cent, liquids (mainly oil) 50 per cent, gas 18 per cent, others (mainly nuclear) 7 per cent. To what extent is the UK self-sufficient in energy supply? How, on the basis of current trends, is the balance between energy supplies likely to change in the UK by the year 2000, and what will be the economic consequences of these changes? (Northern Examinations and Assessment Board 1994, AS level)

4. Drawing on examples of your choice, discuss the extent to which privatization in the UK economy has brought benefits to: (i) consumers of goods and services of privatized industries, (ii) the privatized industries, (iii) the government. (University of Cambridge Local Examinations Syndicate 1994, AS level)

Data Response Question 7

How Mercury and British Telecom compare

This task is based on a question set by the Welsh Joint Education Committee in 1994. The data below includes an adaptation of an article published in the *Financial Times* on 6 March 1991. Study the data carefully, then answer *each* of the questions which follow.

From 1984 until 1991 only two companies, British Telecom (now known as BT) and Mercury Communications, were allowed to supply telephone services in the UK. In March 1991 the government announced plans to allow more firms to enter the telecommunications market. It was concerned about BT's 95% share of the domestic telephone market.

The basic problem of increasing competition is the cost of installing cables, amounting to several hundred pounds per house. BT already has cables to most British homes. Users have to buy a special phone to use the Mercury system.

The principle of 'equal access' is seen as vital to create competition. BT would be forced to allow other companies to use its lines (as Mercury currently does). Each company would have a short code which the caller would dial before the main phone number. The caller

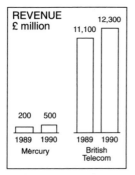

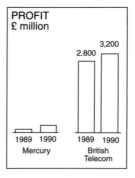

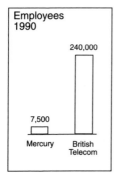

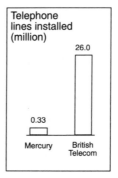

would therefore be able to choose between different suppliers without needing to buy a new phone.

In Hull, where equal access already exists, Mercury has a much higher market share than in the rest of the country. It is argued that equal access would create genuine competition in the domestic telephone market.

Another way of encouraging new entrants (apart from BT and Mercury) would be to allow them to use their telephone lines to transmit cable television programmes. BT and Mercury will not be allowed to supply cable television until at least 2001.

1. Using the data, compare BT and Mercury's (a) size, (b) success. [3,3 marks]
2. Explain the possible difficulties of increasing competition in the supply of domestic telephone services. [7 marks]
3. Why should 'equal access' create advantages for consumers? [6 marks]
4. Why might potential new entrants into the telecommunications market benefit from being allowed to supply cable television programmes? [6 marks]

Conclusion

'Privatization. The word was, to the best of my recollection, David Howell's invention. It is an ugly word – and Margaret disliked it so much that for some time she refused to use it. But none of us could come up with anything better; and as this word, or quite literal translations of it, is now used from Siberia to Patagonia, we may as well stick to it.' Nigel Lawson, *The View From No. 11*

There is certainly room for normative views on privatization. Remember that economists writing in the Press may colour their reports with their own political perspective.

- You can expect hostility from *The Guardian* and *The Observer*.
- You expect sympathy from *The Economist* and *The Times*.

Reading these hardly dispels the 'confused ignorance' that we have been trying to avoid on pages 8 and 31. Is there a summary of positive facts?

From the perspective of the middle of the 1990s, we can see the following quite clearly:

- The early privatizations were a success because the firms involved were already facing competition.
- The utility industries were sold off with priority given to revenue raising rather than to furthering competition.
- The regulators have shown their power and single-mindedness in promoting structural change through deregulation to rectify the governments' shortcomings.
- Consumers now have cheaper gas, electricity and telecoms but higher water bills, in real terms.
- Deregulation of markets forces firms to become more productively efficient.
- Economic theory is upheld by the evidence: competition, rather than ownership, is the key to ensuring higher efficiency.
- Franchising will increasingly improve public sector provision by private sector production.
- Reducing the PSBR and furthering wider share ownership, whilst important, are not major elements to be weighed on the scales of success or failure.
- Seventeen of the UK's Top 100 Companies, based on capital value, are privatized ones.

- The nationalized industries have been annihilated.
- Nationalization replaced market failure.
- Privatization replaces government failure.
- Privatization stands or falls on the promotion of economic efficiency and the welfare gains that accrue to customers in particular and to society in general as gross resource misallocation is reduced.
- Privatization has increased consumer sovereignty in many cases.

Nigel Healey writes, in *Britain's Economic Miracle, Myth or Reality?*:

> *'The intellectual baggage of the postwar consensus, which included nationalisation, state planning and prices and incomes controls, is now disowned by all the mainstream political parties.'*

It is difficult to see how the newly modernized Labour party, led by Tony Blair, will be able to reverse privatization when it comes to power. There is, as yet, no such word in the *Dictionary of Economics* as 'deprivatization'. To try to take BT and BG back into public ownership would cost the Treasury, at current asset valuation, £35 billion. It is impossible to see this being practicable. His success, in 1995, at ridding the 'new' Labour Party, as he calls it, of the Clause 4 millstone – see pages 11 and 15 – illustrates the party's public acceptance of some of the virtues of capitalism. He has stated publicly:

> *'We need a dynamic, modern market economy.'*

Traditionally, parties of the Right and Left have clashed over economics. Much rhetoric is expended by politicians over privatization and even the Archbishop of Canterbury has started to

ANOTHER REDUCTION IN THE COST OF YOUR ELECTRICITY.

We want you, our customers, to continue to share in the success of Eastern Electricity. In your bill today, you will find our Summertime Special – a reduction of £6 in the total cost of your electricity for this quarter.

Our electricity prices will remain at April 1992 levels until at least March 1995. And, as you know, this is the fourth time since May 1993 that we have been able to provide you with a bonus saving.

By purchasing electricity at the lowest possible prices, and by running our company efficiently, we intend to keep on giving you a good deal.

Please accept the Summertime Special with our compliments.

complain about '... the privatization of morality'. A future Labour government will presumably change the powers of the regulators and renationalize the railways.

The last comment should go to Margaret Wilkinson from her book in this series, *Equity and Efficiency*:

> *'Internationally, within mixed though principally capitalist economies the spirit of the age has been towards privatization – less mixture, more capitalism.'*

Index